PRAYER

Jeffrey Pedersen

PRAYER

A Practical Guide to Getting God's Direction

Jeffrey Pedersen

BAAL HAMON PUBLISHERS

AKURE   LONDON   NEW YORK

ISBN-13: 978-1-9999266-0-1

International Correspondence:

www.baalhamonpublishers.com
publishers@baalhamon.com

Contents

Introduction

> *As we search for God, we need to look no further than the very depth of our hearts and minds.*

"Our Father in heaven." (Matthew 6:9). This is the introduction of the "Lord's Prayer" that Jesus taught his disciples to pray. The eternal God of the universe is one that we can know, love, experience, and call upon as our loving Father. God who created the universe is living and real, but he is also loving and personal. He wants us all to experience a loving relationship with him. Prayer allows this relationship to happen. As we pray, we grow in our love and the experience of knowing God in such a special way. Knowing and experiencing the presence of God is our deepest longing. God has come to this world in the most precious way; he became one of us in the divine person of Jesus Christ. Jesus is often referred to as,

"Immanuel- which means, 'God with us.'" (Matthew 1:23)

We can go searching for God, but where will we find him? It isn't that we search for God, as it is that God searches for us. It is God who finds us, and dwells within us. The Apostle Paul writes, "But the righteousness that is by faith says: 'Do not say in your heart, 'Who will ascend into heaven?' (that is, to bring Christ down) or 'Who will descend into the deep?' (that is, to bring Christ up from the dead!). But what does it say? 'The word is near you; it is in your mouth and in your heart,' that is, that word of faith we are proclaiming." (Romans 10:6-8) Jesus said, "The kingdom of God does not come with your careful observation, nor will people say, 'here it is,' or 'There it is,' because the kingdom of God is within you." (Luke 17:20) God establishes his living presence within the believers. "And with that he breathed on them and said, 'Receive the Holy Spirit.'" (John 20:22) God is the potter and we are the clay. "Yet, O Lord, you are our Father. We are the clay, you are the potter, we are all the work of your hand." (Isaiah 64:8) Just as God formed the first man, Adam from the dust, and breathed life into him; so God is our potter who now breathes the resurrection life of Jesus Christ into us, giving new life. Prayer is God breathing his eternal life into us, and dwelling with us. God turns our wayward hearts back to him. In prayer, we offer ourselves to God as his holy temple. The Apostle Paul writes, "Don't you know that you yourselves are God's temple and that God's Spirit lives in you?" (1 Corinthians 3:16) As we search for God, we need to look no further than the very depth of our hearts and minds.

God in this loving relationship transforms us from the inside out. God transforms us back to the original blessedness of being created in his image. This is the work of God, being the potter, and we his clay.

Prayer is God breathing his eternal life into us, and dwelling with us. God turns our wayward hearts back to him. In prayer, we offer ourselves to God as his holy temple.

As we pray, God is renewing our minds. We desire God more than anything and everything. God gives us his heavenly power, his heavenly wisdom, his heavenly attitude, and his heavenly character for life; this supersedes all worldly influences. We desire to be in relationship with God, to follow him, and bring glory to God in all that we do. We can face the challenges, the struggles, and the hurts of life, knowing that we can do all things through him who strengthens us (Philippians 4:13), and that God will work his good purposes in all circumstances (Romans 8:28). God will build us up to be confident, courageous, and victorious people. God gives us a foretaste of the heavenly life on this earth. His presence fills our lives, and gives us a love, a joy, and a peace that surpasses all human understanding (Philippians 4:7).

The Holy Spirit floods our minds with inspiration. As the risen Jesus breathed upon the disciples, they received resurrection life. This breath inspires people. Inspire means to breathe in. As we breathe in the spiritual inspiration of God, we are inspired to do various things. I remember sitting at a conference, where the Holy Spirit flooded my mind with the inspiration to write my book, "River Reflections." I had nothing to write on except my paper coffee cup. I jotted all of my ideas on the cup. I still have the cup in my office; I call it my inspiration cup.

As we pray, the Holy Spirit gives us a passion to be the church, living the vision of being "God's Holy City, the new Jerusalem, coming down from heaven from God." (Revelation 21:2) The Holy Spirit will burn passionately in us. The Holy Spirit is a holy fire that continues to burn brighter and brighter. Like the burning bush that Moses witnessed (Exodus 3:2), the Holy Spirit is eternal and cannot burn out. A fear that is often held by members of the church is, "We don't want to burn anybody out." Would we rather see them rust out? When the Holy Spirit has taken hold of our person, and we dedicate our lives to God, the fire and passion grows. Our roots become grounded deep into God's soil, and our branches grow high into the air, bearing the spiritual fruit that God has purposed for his church. The church will be the city on a hill shinning its light throughout the world. (Matthew 5:14)

As we pray, the Holy Spirit is calling all believers together as the praying church. We gather together to worship God, to be a witness of God's saving grace to all people, to instruct people in God's word, and to be diligent in serving God.

The church gathers for worship. Worship is our spiritual community center. As we read in John 4, we hear of the woman going to the water well, the community center to draw water. As she went to draw water for her physical body, she received the spiritual life in Jesus. Jesus is the heavenly well that brings salvation-life. The church gathers around Jesus, receiving spiritual life through hearing God's Word and receiving the Holy Sacraments of Baptism and Communion. We gather around his banqueting table and have fellowship with God and one another. The words community and communion mean, "Togetherness". It is always the intent of God to bring us together as a community.

The Holy Spirit is always developing the individual to serve the greater whole of the church and society. The Christian believer who is filled with the Holy Spirit has received the salvation of God, and is completely satisfied. The believer now is always asking, "What do I put into the community?" Christian believers are not wondering, how can I drain the community of its resources? That is selfishness. The Holy Spirit has now turned the believer to look outwardly to the needs of others. People will always get out of what they put into something. People will say, "I get the most out of life, when I put the most into life." People will experience so much joy in serving God and others. The **JOY** principle is putting **J**esus first, **O**thers second, and **Y**ourself third.

The Christian believer who receives the breath of the risen savior, Jesus, will experience eternal life with God, now and forever more.

The Holy Spirit is always developing the individual to serve the greater whole of the church and society.

To further define our relationship with God, we use the word covenant. God is a covenant maker. A covenant is a contracted relationship between two or more people. It is God who initiates the covenant. He does this by saving his people. The people then respond in faithful obedience to him. Examples of Old Testament covenants are: Noah, Abraham, Moses, Joshua, and David. God has fulfilled all the Old Testament covenants, the law, and the prophecies, as he has now established a New Covenant in his Son, Jesus. Jesus died on the cross and is arisen from the dead. It is by his blood that the old covenants have been fulfilled and the new covenant is established. We receive the salvation of God in our Baptisms. (1 Peter 3:21; Romans 6:3-4) We receive the salvation of God in Holy Communion. (Luke 22:20) As we live in this covenant, we are nurtured in God's Word. (John 8:31-32; Romans 10:17)

We live in the covenant that God has established with us daily. We daily confess our sins and receive his forgiveness. We pray for the Holy Spirit to give us the inspiration and empowerment to live a godly life in each day. In this covenant we live with the certain hope and promise of eternal life. God gives promises in his covenant. He gives the promises of always being with us (Matthew 28:20), the forgiveness of sins (Matthew 26:28), and eternal life (John 14:2).

A prayerful life is our living in the covenantal relationship that God has established.

Prayer

---

*It is important that we have
a discipline for prayer time.
There are no limits to how
many times we go to our
prayer closet.*

"Here I am! I stand at the door and knock. If anyone hears my voice and opens the door, I will come in and eat with him, and he with me." (Revelation 3:20)

Prayer is our communication with God. God speaks to us through his Word, and we speak to God through our prayers. Prayer is key in knowing God. The more we communicate with God, the deeper the relationship becomes. It is in our communication with God, we have Holy Communion. We feed on God's living Word and we offer ourselves to God in prayer.

God is not a theological concept or a religion. Jesus came into the world not to start a new religion, for the world has enough religions. Jesus came to fulfill God's Word, and be in an intimate relationship with God, the Father. Our life with God needs to be more than going through the motions of traditions and rituals, and the Bible needs to be seen as more than a legalistic rulebook of do's and don'ts. God has fulfilled all the old covenants, and has established a new covenant in his son, Jesus.

God has created humanity to live in relationship with him. Why? Because God loves us. Love is the impetus that moves people in relationships. Jesus stands at the door and knocks, hoping that we will open the door. When we open the door, Jesus will come in and have fellowship with us. God does not want us to just know about him, but rather he wants us to know him. This relationship begins with prayer. We pray, asking God to come into our lives. A man falling in love with a woman wants to be with her all the time. As the man and woman spend more time together, they grow into a deeper and more committed relationship. God loves us, and as we spend time in prayer, our love for God continues to increase more and more.

Just as God is more than an inanimate theological concept, so we as humans created in God's image are spiritual. Humanity has invented physical robots, and computers that think on a high level. One day I was asking an electronic/computer device questions, for which it was able to give me the answers. I then would ask personal questions like, "What makes you sad?" "What makes you happy?" "Who do you love?" The answer to all of these questions was, "I can't answer that." The robot with the computer brain can think on a very high level, and can physically act, but yet the robot is not living. It does not have a soul or spirit. The difference between the created robot and people is that, people are created in the image of God and living; while the computer is not. Our soul hungers and thirsts for God. Prayer brings God into the very depth of our soul.

Our life with God needs to be more than going through the motions of traditions and rituals, and the Bible needs to be seen as more than a legalistic rulebook of do's and don'ts.

Access to God

"Therefore, since we have been justified through faith, we have peace with God through our Lord Jesus Christ, through whom we have gained access by faith into this grace in which we now stand." (Romans 5:1-2)

Why is there a door? Shouldn't there be open access to God? It was God's original blessing to not have doors, but rather a relationship of openness to share. God wants a relationship based on love, not on control, manipulation, or coercion. With love there is a risk. We may love someone, but that someone may not reciprocate that love. That is the chance that God took with humanity. God placed a tree in the Garden of Eden where humanity was free to choose to love God or to leave God. This tree was forbidden for the man and woman to eat from. If they ate from this tree, they would die. Why? Because it would be humanity saying to God, "No, we do not want to live in a relationship with you. We don't want to be the stewards of the earth, but rather we want to be the owner of creation and life. We want to be God."

Humanity's decision was one of closing the door to God. This was not God's plan or desire for humanity, but rather humanity's fatal decision. The consequence for humanity's sin is death. (Genesis 3:3, Romans 6:23) God drove the couple, Adam and Eve, out of the Garden of Eden, and had an angel with a flaming sword placed at the door preventing them from entering in. Humanity is now on a path leading to death, rather than the one that leads to life.

Humanity now claims ownership to what does not belong to them. In this attitude, they oppose God, and work at ridding creation and life from God. Humanity's attitude says, "We don't need God, we know what is best for us, and we don't need God messing around in our business!" This is the story Jesus tells of the wicked stewards in Matthew 21:33-44. In this story God is assigning humanity to be the stewards of the earth. The stewards rebel, even killing the messengers that God has sent to them. Finally, God sends his Son, thinking they would show respect to him. Instead, they killed his Son, Jesus, believing their actions will result in their being the heirs. "But when the tenants saw the Son, they said to each other, 'this is the heir. Come let's kill him and take his inheritance.' So they took him and threw him out of the vineyard and killed him." (Matthew 21:38-39)

Humanity crucified Jesus, but God had a loving plan. It is through the death and resurrection of Jesus, God has given salvation to the world. "For God so loved the world that he gave his only begotten son, so that whoever believes in him shall not perish but have eternal life." (John 3:16)

All of humanity is in the same status, as we read in Romans 3:23, "For all have sinned and fallen short of the glory of God." As we read further in Romans 6:23, "The wages of sin is death, but the free gift of God is eternal life in Jesus Christ."

When Jesus was crucified the curtain in the Temple was torn in two. (Matthew 27:51) The curtain in the Temple was the wall that separated the Holy of Holies where God dwelt, from the Holy Place where the priests would be. Now that the curtain has been torn in two, humanity has access to God. There is nothing that separates us from the love of God in Christ Jesus. (Romans 8:39) The door blocking paradise has been removed. (Revelation 22:14) This is important because there will be a judgment for all of us. This is the day when God will judge people to heaven or hell. When we live our lives in God, we live in the joy and peace of being in his blessed assurance. We love God, and we long to be with him in paradise.

As we pray, God has opened the door to paradise. We have access to God. In prayer, we open the door of our hearts to God.

The Heavenly Invasion

Even though this division between God and humanity exists, God still loves us, and has given his gracious offer of friendship to us. He does this by sending his Son. Jesus was born in a stable on the edge of Bethlehem, because there was no room in the Bethlehem Inn. This represented humanity's "No Vacancy" sign to God. "God, we don't want you in our world!" God does slip in through the crack of the back door.

As Jesus was going about his public ministry, he was doing it outside of the mainstream of life. He taught on the hillsides, seashores, and in people's homes. He stayed away from the mainline teachers of the law, the synagogues, and Jerusalem where the Temple was. Jesus stayed in the homes of those who would receive him, and used the resources that people provided. Even the donkey that Jesus rode into Jerusalem on Palm Sunday was borrowed. Jesus being the owner of all creation is the humble servant, being a good steward of all God would provide. Jesus was crucified on a wooden cross. Jesus was buried in a borrowed rich man's tomb. It was once again the choice of humanity to reject God, reinforcing their misguided idea that they are the owners of creation and life.

This is the heavenly invasion of Jesus slipping through the crack of the back door, flooding the world with his love, grace, and mercy. God has filled the believers with the radiance of his presence. God has given salvation to all people who have come to believe and receive him.

Prayer as Watchfulness

Prayer is being watchful. When Jesus was born in Bethlehem, the angel appeared to the shepherds. The shepherds were the watchmen. They would remain vigilant as they would watch and protect their sheep from predators and thieves. They were out in the country, so they would be watchful for pursuing armies who wanted to attack the city. They would be the ones to warn the city that an attack is coming, to prepare for battle. They were the ones to stay awake and see the Lord's appearing.

Prayer is how we stay awake spiritually. When Jesus was in the Garden of Gethsemane, he went to pray, and he called his disciples to pray with him; but they could not stay awake. (Luke 22:45-46) Prayer makes us attentive to God. We keep watchful for his appearing each day, and what he has called us to do. We keep alert in prayer as we wait for the second coming of Jesus Christ. (Matthew 24:42)

Prayer as opening the Door

Jesus is knocking on our doors. The door that Jesus is referring to is the door of our heart. Our heart represents our greatest value. It is our deepest yearning in life. Our heart is our personal throne. Who sits on our throne? What is our greatest value? Jesus is the one who wants to sit on the throne as our highest value. Jesus does not barge into our lives; he doesn't knock down the door. The handle of the door is on the inside. It is up to us to open the door. Prayer opens the door.

How much does Jesus want to come into our lives? It is like water that is held back by a dam. When the water dam is opened, the water comes rushing through. God is like the water when we open our hearts door to him. God rushes into our lives, filling our whole life with his person. God wants to enter into every part of our person. He comes in and has fellowship with us. In prayer, we let Jesus into our lives, and we give him permission to sit upon our hearts' throne. Jesus is our savior and Lord.

Prayer is being watchful . . . Prayer is how we stay awake spiritually . . . Prayer makes us attentive to God.

Prayer is Relationship

When we pray, we are in relationship with God. We are living in the purpose that God intended for our lives. We can approach God as our loving father. Jesus gave a model prayer, and taught us to pray, "Our Father who art in heaven." Just as loving parents have relationships with their children, so God has a loving relationship with us.

As we read in John 15, Jesus describes the relationship with God as intimate as a vine to its branches. Jesus said, "We abide together in God's love."

(Verse 9) It is God's love that binds us together with cords that cannot be broken. God's love is eternal, indestructible, nurturing, and providing all we need to have a healthy relationship with him and other believers. Jesus says, "As you remain in me, your joy will be complete." (Verse 11) We experience joy when Jesus is at the center of our lives. Jesus no longer calls us slaves, sinners, or forsaken, but rather as his friends. Jesus said, "Greater love has no one than this, that he lay down his life for his friends." (Verse 13) We are in relationship with God as his friends, children, and church.

Prayer as Communication

When in relationships with others, we take the time to communicate with them. We communicate through our speaking and listening. We speak to God in prayer, as we would speak to a loving parent or friend. We also listen to God in prayer. What is God speaking to our hearts? What is God speaking to us through his Word? What is God speaking through other believers?

We also communicate through our posture. When we have our hands lifted high, we are communicating our openness to God. This is an expression of praise. When we pray with our heads bowed, we are communicating humility before him. We are saying, "God you are the Creator, and I am the created. I submit my person to your lordship."

The main point of prayer is simply being in relationship with the Father. We take the time to spend with God every day. We can talk to God about anything. Everyone can pray. It doesn't take a master theologian or someone who has been a Christian for a number of years to pray. Prayer is something that everyone can do.

Prayer Closet

Jesus taught, "But when you pray, go into your room, close the door and pray to your Father, who is unseen." (Matthew 6:6) When we pray, we are to go to our closet. Our closet represents our personal place. So often, people use their closets to do things that won't be seen by other people. People go to their closets to do things that are not morally sound. People may say, "What I do in my closet is my business." What we do in our closet does affect our person, how we live our lives, and our attitude toward God and others. Some people come out of their closets willfully, while other times what they are doing in the closet is exposed in an embarrassing way. What we do in our private life expresses itself in our public life. We need our closets to be sacred places of honor. As we honor God in our private lives, God will be then honored in our public lives.

What Jesus is saying is, "What you are to be doing in your closet is praying." Time spent praying in our closets will give us passion for God that leads to a passionate life. Do not allow the Devil to come in and set-up shop. Make your closet the place where you meet God, and see how God will work his heavenly wonder in your life. Prayer uplifts us to experience more than what this world can ever offer. God enriches our lives with heavenly splendor.

Prayer as Spiritual Exercise

God has created us to have our body, soul, and mind. As a marathon runner, one disciplines oneself to be physically fit. The runner must take the time daily to exercise and optimize his potentials. As a student, one takes the time to exercise one's mind, and one learns a subject, growing in the knowledge and making the most of the good mind God has given. The same is true with our spirit. We need to take the time to pray. The more we pray, the stronger we become spiritually, and our relationship with God grows. God opens our life to all of his creative and redeeming work in the world. The more we pray, the more we will want to be in prayer, and our faith life will continue to develop and mature into a Christ-like person.

We also communicate through our posture. When we have our hands lifted high, we are communicating our openness to God. This is an expression of praise. When we pray with our heads bowed, we are communicating humility before him.

Problems that people have in prayer are:

1) *Having a relationship with God is contrary to our human nature.* Because of the fall to sin, we want to be our own God, so praying is unnatural to our human nature.

2) *We become tired spiritually.* It is easy to become spiritually lazy, just as we can be physically and academically lazy. We have a tendency to fall asleep spiritually. Prayer is what keeps us awake.

3) *We are too busy to pray.* We can become so busy with the cares of this world that we do not have the time to pray. Great people of faith like Martin Luther, John Calvin, and John Wesley would say, "I'm too busy not to pray." When you feel stressed and anxious about your busy day with all of its demands, take time to pray, and God will order your day like nothing else can do.

How often should we pray? The Apostle Paul writes in 1 Thessalonians 5:17, "Pray continually." We are to always have our minds on God, and we meditate on him always. We are continually asking for his counsel and advice in all matters of life. It is important that we have a discipline for prayer time. There are no limits to how many times we go to our prayer closet. We can go to our prayer closet in the morning as we start our day. We can go to our prayer closet during the day, as we are experiencing the height of what is happening. We can close our day in prayer as well. The main thing is that we take the time each day to pray.

The length of time is not what matters, but we pray as long as we need to share what is on our mind and as we listen to what God is speaking to us.

Having time in our prayer closet generally consists of spending time in God's word (the Bible), reading a devotional based on a Bible reading, and praying. This is where we open and bear our hearts to God.

The main point of prayer is simply being in relationship with the Father. . . . What we do in our private life expresses itself in our public life...Time spent praying in our closets will give us passion for God that leads to a passionate life.

QUESTIONS

1. What makes for effective communication?
2. What is prayer in relationship to God?
3. How do we have access to God?
4. How has God entered the world?
5. What do you watch for in prayer?
6. How do we open our hearts door to God?
7. How does prayer allow a relationship with God?
8. Where is your prayer closet?
9. How do we exercise our spirit?
10. Why is praying sometimes difficult?

Prayer and the Holy Spirit

As we pray, we are anointed with the Holy Spirit. Our lives are filled to overflowing, spilling over to those around us.

"Every time I feel the spirit moving in my heart I will pray!"

As a freshman college student, I made the commitment that I would have my morning devotions. My morning devotions consisted of reading my Bible and praying. One morning as I was having my devotions, I had this feeling that came over me and within me. The feeling was radiant, peaceful, embracing, and inspiring. I wasn't looking for any kind of a spiritual/psychological experience. As I went about my day, I didn't think too much about the experience, until the next morning as I was having my devotions. The feeling came again, as it has every day since then. I didn't understand what was happening, so I confided in a Christian who explained to me, "What you are feeling is the Holy Spirit coming upon you and filling you." I realized that the Holy Spirit is real, and that the real presence of God desired to be in my life.

John Wesley was a reformer and founder of the Methodist Church. He was a brilliant preacher, leading thousands of people to faith. Yet, he didn't feel a strong faith within himself. It happened one day as he was listening to a teacher read Martin Luther's, Preface On Romans at the Aldersgate in London, England. It was there the Holy Spirit warmed his heart. It was at this moment that he received a strong passionate faith.

The Holy Spirit Gives Us Passion

Jesus had a passionate love for humanity, as he suffered and died on the cross. This is the amazing love and grace of God. It is this passion that flows from the cross into our lives, giving us passion for God. Just as the Holy Spirit was moving over the waters in creation, the Holy Spirit is moving through the waters of baptism making us a new creation in Jesus Christ. The water life of God flows through the cross and into our lives. The waters continue to flow through us into the world. As we are blessed, we are now to be a blessing to others.

The prophet Jeremiah was punished for preaching God's word. From a personal perspective, he wanted to stop preaching to avoid any further punishment. He continued to preach. These are the words of Jeremiah, "But if I say, 'I will not mention him or speak anymore in his name,' his word is in my heart like a fire, a fire shut up in my bones. I am weary of holding it in, indeed, I cannot." (Jeremiah 20:9) The Holy Spirit was Jeremiah's motivation to be passionate about God's work. Even though it caused Jeremiah much pain, preaching was his passion in life. God gives us the passion to be his people and to be about his calling. We pray that God gives us the passion to be his people, even when we suffer for it.

When Jesus arose from the dead, he breathed on the disciples the Holy Spirit. He breathed on them the resurrection life of God. The risen Christ dwells in the hearts of the believers in the Holy Spirit, empowering them to be the church of God in this world. "And with that he breathed on them and said, 'Receive the Holy Spirit.'" (John 20:22) Prayer is receiving the Holy Spirit- the breath of God, the life of God, and the unity of God.

The Holy Spirit will give us the passion to obey God's commandments, love our neighbors, trust in God's salvation promise, and live in the unity with the Heavenly Father. The Holy Spirit is the passionate fire in our hearts. We need to let the Holy Spirit burn like a fire in a lamp, and let the radiance of it be a witness to the world. The rays of God's light that shines through us, are our good works. Jesus said, "Let your light shine before men, that they may see your good deeds and praise your Father in heaven." (Matthew 5:16)

The Filling of the Holy Spirit

Acts 2:1-4 states, "When the day of Pentecost came, they were all together in one place. Suddenly a sound like a blowing of a violent wind came from heaven, and filled the whole house where they were sitting. They saw what seemed to be tongues of fire that separated and came to rest on each of them. All of them were filled with the Holy Spirit and began to speak in other tongues as the Spirit enabled them." This fulfills the prophecy spoken by Joel (Joel 2:28-32), "The Holy Spirit will come upon all flesh." It was on the day of Pentecost that the Holy Spirit came upon the believers of Jesus like a rush of a mighty wind. Pentecost means, "Fiftieth Day." It was a major Jewish festival held fifty days after the Passover festival. For Christians, it was fifty days following the resurrection of Jesus.

Jesus told his disciples that he was going to leave them, and that he was going to send the Holy Spirit who will be the counselor. The Christian church believes in God the Father, God the Son, and God the Holy Spirit. They are one in substance, mind, and purpose; they make up the Holy Trinity. When the Holy Spirit comes upon the believers, the Holy Spirit fills, and becomes infused in the believers. It will not help a thirsty person to simply hold a bottle of water, and believe that the water can quench his thirst. It is when the person drinks the water that physical life is nurtured. Like water to the body, so the Holy Spirit brings our spiritual self to life. As the Apostle Paul writes in Galatians 2:20, "I have been crucified with Christ, it is no longer I who live, but it is Christ who dwells within me." Christ dwells within the believers by the Holy Spirit. Paul also writes in 1 Corinthians 3:16, "You are the temple of the Holy Spirit." God dwells in Heaven as well as earth. "Heaven is his throne, and the earth his footstool." (Isaiah 61:1) God's throne on earth is the hearts of the believers. It is easy to think that God's throne is in some beautiful cathedral, but the throne that God wants to be seated on is the throne of our heart.

Receiving the Holy Spirit

How do we receive the Holy Spirit? Is there some formula that we need to know? Do we have to be a pastor or a priest to receive the Holy Spirit? Are we to have a certain level of understanding of the Bible? Does it have to do with ethnicity or social status? As we read in Luke 11, Jesus gives instruction in prayer. Jesus said in verse 13, "If you then, though you are evil, know how to give good gifts to your children, how much more will your Father in heaven give the Holy Spirit to those who ask him!" God wants to bless all people with the Holy Spirit, all we need to do is ask in prayer. Just open your heart to God, and pray, "Come, Holy Spirit, fill my heart and life this day." The Holy Spirit will come and fill your life as Jesus has promised. If people are wondering what to pray for, pray for the Holy Spirit. It is the life of God entering into your person. What God wants from us more than anything is to be in relationship with us. Much like a young man who loves a young woman, the two of them want to be in each other's presence all the time. As they are in each other's presence, they continue to grow in their relationship. As the Holy Spirit fills our hearts we long for and desire God more and more.

Spiritual Bond of God's Love

Jesus said, "As the Father has loved me, so have I loved you. Now remain in my love. If you obey my commands, you will remain in my love, just as I have obeyed my Father's commands and remain in his love. I have told you this so that my joy may be in you and that your joy may be complete. My command is this: Love one another as I have loved you." (John 15:9-12)

The relationship that God has with us is filled with joy. We experience the fullness of joy in him. Jesus calls us to obey the commandments of God. The commandments can be obeyed through love. We love God, and then we love one another. As sin has separated us from God and has fractured the relationships with others, so love bonds us together with God and our neighbors. This is all made possible through the cross of Jesus. The cross stands at the center of our relationships with God and one another. In the cross we have pardon and peace, redemption and reconciliation, and healing and restoration. There is the vertical axis of the cross, this represents our relationship with God. In the cross, we are reconciled to him. The horizontal axis represents our blessed relationships with each other through Christ.

In Jesus Christ, we have been bonded together in his love. We experience the joy of being the church. As we gather to pray, God is present. It is in our praying that we are bonded spiritually. The strongest bonds are always spiritual. The strongest bond is God's love. I have a friend who is from Africa. One night we were praying together, and I felt the Holy Spirit upon me as we were praying. At a certain time, I stopped praying. My African friend became angry with me. He said, "How can you stop praying when the Holy Spirit is upon us?" I didn't know that he was also feeling the Holy Spirit's presence. I learned that night, that you continue to pray as long as you feel the Holy Spirit's presence.

Together we are experiencing the Holy Spirit who calls us together to be the body of Christ, the church. God inspires us to have faith, and calls us to action and life. The church is to be active, serving the world in ministry and mission. The church is bonded together in the Holy Spirit. John writes, "And this is his command to believe in the name of his son, Jesus Christ, and to love one another as he commanded us. Those who obey his commands live in him and he in them. And this is how we know that he lives in us: We know it by the Spirit he gave us." (1 John 3:23-24)

The Work of the Holy Spirit

As we read in John 16:5-11, Jesus gives us instruction of what the Holy Spirit will do. The first thing is the Holy Spirit will convict us of sin. The Holy Spirit will convince us that we need a savior. The second thing the Holy Spirit will do is convince us that Jesus Christ is the savior that God has given. In Jesus, we have the full expiation of our sins. God is completely satisfied with his loving sacrifice. It is by Jesus, we have complete redemption of our sins, and our relationship with God has been completely restored. The third thing the Holy Spirit will do is sanctify us. Sanctification is the Holy Spirit's work to make us holy people of God. "But just as he who called you is holy, so be holy in all you do; for it is written: 'Be holy, because I am holy.'" (1 Peter 1:15-16) This means that God is in the process of transforming us into his holy people. The Holy Spirit will help us grow in faith, instruct us in the truth, and lead us in the purposes for which he has called us. It is the Holy Spirit, God's presence that will continue to nurture us in fervent love for him.

Always With Us

As we read in John 14:15-18, Jesus teaches us that he will not leave us orphaned. Jesus was sharing with his disciples that he must leave, but will not leave them orphaned. The disciples experienced grief by Jesus' words. The disciples had left their homes, families, and work to follow Jesus; now he was going to leave them. An orphan is a child who has no parents. They were feeling orphaned in their faith. Jesus' teaching was to explain that as he ascends back to heaven, that he will send the Holy Spirit who will be with them always.

It is the Holy Spirit who will guide them in all truth. Jesus is the way, the truth, and the life of God. The Holy Spirit will bring back to the remembrance all that Jesus has taught. This remembrance is kept for us in the Holy Bible. The Apostle Paul refers to the Bible as being the sword of the Holy Spirit who will give us instruction in the truth of Jesus Christ. (Ephesians 6:17)

It is easy to think that God's throne is in some beautiful cathedral, but the throne that God wants to be seated on is the throne of our heart.

Jesus refers to the Holy Spirit as being the counselor who will guide you in all the truth. A counselor is someone who advises someone else. The counselor advises according to the truth. What is the standard or template that a counselor uses to determine what is normal from what is abnormal, what is right from wrong, what is true from what is false, and what is good from what is bad? That is always the question for the counselor. For whatever template is used will determine this. For Christians, our standard and template is Jesus. Jesus takes us from what is false, bad, wrong, and abnormal; and transforms us to be more and more in his likeness. This is the Holy Spirit working in our lives. The Apostle Paul wrote, "Do not conform any longer to the pattern of this world, but be transformed by the renewing of your mind. Then you will be able to test and approve what God's will is-his good, pleasing and perfect will." (Romans 12:2)

The Holy Spirit Prays For Us

The Holy Spirit is of the same substance as the Father and the Son. When Jesus promised to be with us until the end of the age, we wonder how does he do this? He sends the Holy Spirit. The Holy Spirit is likened to the wind. Just like the air is omnipresent in the world, so the Holy Spirit is omnipresent. Just as people around the world are all breathing the air, God now offers his presence everywhere in the person of the Holy Spirit. People can be filled and pray everywhere in the world. I once had a friend who asked, "How can God be hearing the prayers of people in China and also with us here?"

Just as people in China are breathing the air, so we are. All seven billion people in the world are breathing the air, so all seven billion people can pray, and God hears their prayers.

As we read in Romans 8:26-28, "In the same way, the Spirit helps us in our weakness. We do not know what we ought to pray for, but the Spirit himself intercedes for us with groans that words cannot express. And he who searches our hearts knows the mind of the Spirit, because the Spirit intercedes for the saints in accordance to God's will." The Apostle Paul says that the divine is within us (The Holy Spirit), prays to the divine (The Heavenly Father).

As a child, I would ask my parents for many things. Sometimes they would give me what I asked for and other times they would not. My parents in their wisdom and love for me knew what I needed better than I knew myself. God who knows our innermost person, answers prayers according to his will, in what we need. A gift of the Holy Spirit is praying in tongues. This is the Holy Spirit praying to God, interceding on our behalf.

The Apostle Paul writes in Ephesians 1:13-14, "Having believed, you were marked in him with a seal, the promised Holy Spirit, who is a deposit guaranteeing our inheritance until the redemption of those who are God's possession-to the praise of his glory." The Holy Spirit dwelling within us is God, who gives us salvation. The Holy Spirit's presence is an official seal of God, and is like earnest money on a house. God makes his claim upon us as his children.

Prayer and Behavior

The words of King Solomon in Ecclesiastes 3:11, "He has also set eternity in the hearts of men." God has given us an innate sense. God has given us the innate sense for eternity. Eternity is a blessing that all people long for. All people, whether they are believers or not have a sense of eternity. God has placed eternity in our hearts. Our spirit longs and yearns for the fulfillment of this desire. That fulfillment comes through the death and resurrection of Jesus.

As we live our lives in this world, the Holy Spirit gives us the innate desires of God. We have the inner drive to do what Jesus wants us to do. I once had a farmer come to me in a bit of anger and frustration. He said, "I told my son to do his chores." His son sassed at him asking, "If I do my chores, what is my reward?" The son was learning behavior modification through rewards and punishments. In this development, outward variables are used. The Farmer, says, "If this is my son's attitude, we are not going to get anything done." God gives us innate desires, and motivates us to do the right things without any rewards or punishments attached to them. As Christians, we desire to do what God desires for us, our behavior is motivated by the Holy Spirit. The Holy Spirit transforms our hearts to the unity of the Heavenly Father.

We grow to be more like Jesus in our lives. He is the image and example of God in our world. The church is to become more like him. As a grade school student learning to write, I was given lined paper to practice writing the letters of the alphabet. At the top of the page was the perfect example of the letter. I would practice making my letters to look like the modeled example, but I never mastered the perfection. The more I practiced, the better my letters became. That is what God does for us in prayer. The Holy Spirit continues to transform our lives to be more like Jesus. When this growth of holiness happens, we have a deeper desire to worship God, and to look outside of ourselves in serving our neighbors. Jesus life was poured out for all of us. We receive this eternal flow of Heavenly life, as we pray for the Holy Spirit to enter into our lives.

"You anoint my head with oil, my cup overflows." (Psalm 23:5) God floods the world with his love. As we pray, we are anointed with the Holy Spirit. Our lives are filled to overflowing, spilling over to those around us. The Holy Spirit's overflowing anointing is our ministry and mission in the world. Our lives become an outpouring of God's love, bringing healing to a broken world. It is God's desire to make the world whole. Let your life be filled to overflowing with the love and grace of God.

Each day pray, "Come Holy Spirit, fill my life, that I may love you more and more. Amen."

QUESTIONS

1. Who is the Holy Spirit?
2. When did God give the Holy Spirit?
3. How do we receive the Holy Spirit?
4. How does God bind relationships?
5. What is the work of the Holy Spirit?
6. How does Jesus continue to be with us?

7. What is the Holy Spirit's sword?
8. What is the Christians template of truth?
9. How does the Holy Spirit pray for us?
10. How is the Holy Spirit a seal?

Prayer for the Will of God

Christians aligned with God's will know they have been created special. God has a relational purpose with them

Jesus taught us to pray the Lord's Prayer. One of the petitions of the Lord's Prayer is, "Thy will be done on earth, as it is in heaven." (Matthew 6:10) Heaven is God's throne and the earth is his footstool. (Isaiah 61:1) God is always working to build up his kingdom in this world. God's kingdom is the Christian church on earth, as it is in heaven. It crosses all physical and social boundaries. God wants all people to be his church, the assembly of believers.

God's will is being done in heaven, but it is also God's desire to have his will be done on this earth. God has created humanity to live in harmony with him. We must be in synchronization with our creator. A fish belongs in the water, and not on the land. Humanity living apart from God is like the fish trying to live on land. It just doesn't work out. We defy God's natural order for creation, obedience to his law, and God's plan of reconciliation. We are created to worship God and to follow in his good instruction. This is the blessed life that God desires for all of us. We may live in peace with all of creation, and have prosperity with all peoples, tribes, and nations.

God's Will for Jesus

John 3:16, "For God so loved the world that he gave his one and only Son, that whoever believes in him shall not perish but have eternal life." God's will for Jesus is that he is the savior of humanity. God did not send his son into the world to save only a certain privileged few, but it is God's will and intention to save the world through Christ. God's love is not partial, but rather full. It is God's will to save all people, and that includes you. This is not to suggest universal salvation, but it is God's desire that all will receive salvation in Jesus Christ.

Jesus said, "For I have come down from heaven not to do my will but to do the will of him who sent me. And this is the will of him who sent me, that I shall lose none of all that he has given me, but raise them up at the last day. For my Father's will is that everyone who looks to the Son and believes in him shall have eternal life, and I will raise him up at the last day." (John 6:38-40) Jesus was sent to do God's will. God's will for Jesus was that he would die on the cross for humanity's sins, and bring salvation (eternal life) for all who come to believe in him.

The Apostle Peter spoke, "All who call upon the name of the Lord will be saved." (Acts 2:21)

God's Will is Not Always Easy

In Matthew 26:36-46, Jesus is agonizing in the Garden of Gethsemane. This was the moment prior to Jesus' arrest. He was praying to the Heavenly Father for strength, as he was being tempted by the Devil to give up God's plan of bringing redemption through the cross. Jesus was praying that the cup of suffering might pass from him. He prayed, "God, not my will, but your will be done." It was God's will that Jesus go the way of the cross, and Jesus was obedient to God's will.

Jesus also called his disciples three times to wait in prayer for an hour. Each time they fell asleep. If the disciples didn't keep vigilant in prayer, they would not be able to withstand the temptation to fall away from Jesus, as he would be arrested. Shortly after this, Jesus was arrested by Roman soldiers, was given a mock trial by the religious leaders, was sentenced to death by the Judean governor Pontius Pilate, and was taken to the place of the skull to be crucified. Jesus disciples did flee for their lives.

It is desirous to think that God's will is always a life of pleasure. We may think it is the easy path, where everything falls into place. So many times in life as we are praying to God, asking for guidance in critical times, discerning God's will, we discover that God's call is not always the easy way. A young man had the choice of taking one of two jobs that were offered him. Both jobs paid very well, and were in very nice cities. If he were to choose the one job, he would be surrounded by Christians who shared so many of the same interests, while working in the other job he would be surrounded by unbelievers. It seemed obvious that he would accept the first job opportunity, but as he prayed, God was calling him to the second. He thought his Christian witness would be stronger among the unbelievers.

So many times in life as we are praying to God, asking for guidance in critical times, discerning God's will, we discover that God's call is not always the easy way.

The Apostle Paul writes in Romans 12:1-2, "Therefore, I urge you, brothers, in view of God's mercy, to offer your bodies as living sacrifices holy and pleasing to God-this is your spiritual act of worship. Do not conform any longer to the pattern of this world, but be transformed by the renewing of your mind. Then you will be able to test and approve what God's will is-his good, pleasing and perfect will." It is human nature to be selfish and look inwardly, but it is God's will for us to look outside of self to the concerns of others. A Christian is continually renewing and being transformed into the likeness of Jesus who poured out his life for all humanity. Jesus said, "If anyone would come after me, he must deny himself and take up his cross and follow me." (Matthew 16:24) The Holy Spirit is transforming our lives through Jesus. We are to bear witness of Jesus work on the cross:

> 1) *We are to proclaim the good news of salvation through Jesus.*
>
> 2) *We are to strive for justice and peace in the world.*
>
> 3) *We are to pour out our Christian love and serve our neighbors in need.*

Paul also wrote in Romans 8:28, "And we know that in all things God works the good of those who love him, who have been called according to his purpose." As we reflect upon this verse, we understand that we need to align our lives with the will and purposes of God. When we do, God will redeem all of life's experiences, the good, the bad, and the indifferent. God's goodness is working in us. The godly good is: godly character, godly wisdom, godly strength, and godly works. We have dedicated our lives for the causes of Christ.

Where is God? Is God in heaven? Yes, but he also dwells in our hearts. God engages in our lives, not only in the good times, but also in the very difficult times. Because God is with us at all times, he can use all of life's experiences for his redemption and glory. We find meaning and strength as we reflect upon the suffering and death of Jesus, and also his resurrection and life. Jesus descends into the very depth of hell, so that we may ascend into the very heights of heaven. (1 Peter 3:19) Jesus brings meaning, purpose, and life, out of the darkest circumstances of life.

Divine Providence

So many times, we do not understand why things happen the way they do in a day. As we look back on life, we can understand why certain things have happened, or we find a deep meaning in something that we will never understand. In both cases, we see the footprints of God being evident in our lives. God has worked the events of yesterday and has made something good today.

There has been Theological debate over time about God's divine providence. Since the fall of humanity, one argument is that humanity is on such a chaotic path and that even God doesn't know where humanity is going; that humanity is completely out of control. However, the truth is that God does know where humanity is heading. It is heading for ultimate death.

Another argument is that after the fall of Adam and Eve, humanity has chosen to take a different course. Humanity is now on a cataclysmic course that is heading for disaster. In the end, sinful humanity will progress to the point of doing itself in. An example of this is war. Humanity has the weaponry capable of destroying the earth. A second example would be the depletion of the environment that God called humanity to be the stewards of. A third example would be the technology to undermine and destroy the sociological structures that are in place.

Humanity's social engagements are now being replaced by robotic and social media technology. Humanity is becoming disengaged with one another; we are losing personal touch and conversation. We are growing to be impersonal in our interaction with others.

If we pray for selfish things, we will be disappointed with not receiving what we ask for, but when we live for the purposes of God, we will see prayers answered in amazing ways.

God has created people to walk on a righteous path. We understand that God in his marvelous wonder has created all things, including each one of us. God has placed the billions of galaxies with all of their stars in order. God has created each person unique and special. God has given us light that travels at 186,000 miles per second. God has given us the acorn that is all programmed to die in the soil, and be raised to be a mammoth oak tree. God has made all the intricate systems of our body to work together. God has given us lungs to breathe the air, eyes that can receive light, ears that can receive sound waves, and a three pound brain that can process all of this in an intelligent way. God has given to us the physical laws and social laws. When we are obedient to God and compliant with these laws, we all live well in the land.

We can see that something has gone drastically wrong with the world God had created. God has given blessed life, but people kill one another, and hate one another through bullying and gossiping. People steal from one another, have insatiable greed, and desire the lusts of the flesh that lead to sexual immorality; and humanity is consuming the world's resources at an enormous rate. At this point we would say, "The world is not aligned with God's will, but rather is set on an unrighteous path that God did not order." This path would say, "There is no God. There is no purpose to life, since creation is described as being accidental, and there is no culminating purpose." These understandings lead to a world that is hopelessly despondent. The moment Adam and Eve fell to sin, was the moment that God knew he would send his son, Jesus to be the sacrifice. This is amazing love.

Christians aligned with God's will know they have been created special. God has a relational purpose with them, with creation, and with each other; and the Christian people know that life is heading for a hopeful culmination. God desires for us to have eternal life, where there will be no more suffering, brokenness, or death.

Misunderstanding Prayer

As God's people, we can stumble in prayer with good intentions. We may pray to God with many good requests, but yet find that our prayers are not answered.

Even though we don't say it directly, so many times when we reflect on our praying, we are really praying, "My will be done." It is easy to start looking at God as being a Genie who will grant us wishes, or Santa Claus who will give us everything we ask for, no matter how selfish the requests may be.

Sometimes our prayer requests can be selfish and shortsighted. If I were to have a tough day ahead, and I just don't want to face it, I might pray, "God don't let tomorrow happen. Just don't even allow the sun to come up." The next day when the sun comes up, what would I concur? I may say, "If there is a God, God doesn't answer prayer."

I think of sporting events where people on both sides of the competition pray and demand that God would side with their team. This puts God in a tough position, as if God would have any desire to influence the outcome. We need to pray for the Holy Spirit to dwell in us. We should pray, "God let your will be done, help me to do my best. If I win, I praise you and thank you, and help me to show a good attitude in the victory. If I lose, help me to rejoice in the other person's success, help me to have integrity in the defeat, and also, Lord help me to learn from it." In all our efforts, we pray that we can bring glory to God.

God has physical laws and natural cycles placed in creation. Specific things have to happen for the sake of the larger environment that we live in. We may not like it, but there are reasons why natural disasters happen. There are reasons for droughts, floods, earthquakes, hurricanes, and forest fires. These are not ways that God uses to pick on us, God sees a larger picture to his creative order. Events of creation cannot be judged in a moment, but rather in the context of a longer history. We need to see a larger ecological picture of why they need to happen. An example of this would be the person who prays that it won't rain on his picnic. As this person is praying for a sunny day, a farmer is praying for a rainy day to nourish his crops. We must be thankful for and make the most of each day, whether we have sunshine or rain. God's creative purposes are greater than any individual or moment in time.

A Selfish Will

As we read Matthew 20:20-23, we hear the story of the mother of the sons of Zebedee's coming to make a selfish request. She wanted her sons to sit at Jesus right hand and the left hand in his kingdom. They believed that Jesus was going to defeat the Roman's and usher in a new regime of leadership. She was asking Jesus if her sons could have positions of power when this happens. Jesus came not to establish a worldly kingdom, but rather a heavenly one. Jesus came as the humble servant who would die on a cross for the people. Jesus asked her, "Can they drink the cup that I will drink?" She said, "Yes." Jesus said, "They will, but to sit at my right and left hand is for only God to grant."

A misuse of prayer is a controlling attitude. People can see prayer as a control mechanism. We may try to force God's hand in controlling other people. A father wanted his son to take over the family business. The son has aspirations of becoming a teacher. The father prays, asking God to change his son. When the father's prayer is not being answered, as his son becomes a teacher, he is upset with God.

We do not use prayer for worldly fame and fortune. As people try to gain wealth, they pray to God, hoping they will become very wealthy. They may say, "God wants to give me the abundant life!" (John 10:10) The abundant life that Jesus is referring to is not one of worldly wealth and pleasure, but rather it is a life full of God. The abundant life is being filled with the salvation of Jesus, and the life of the Holy Spirit. It is receiving the richness of heavens presence on earth.

Jesus said, "Again, I tell you that if two of you on earth agree about anything you ask for, it will be done for you by my Father in heaven. For where two or three come together in my name, there am I with them." (Matthew 18:19-20) Jesus made this statement to those who have committed their lives for the causes of God, not people who are seeking selfish ambitions. If we pray for selfish things, we will be disappointed with not receiving what we ask for, but when we live for the purposes of God, we will see prayers answered in amazing ways. God will provide all we need to fulfill his purposes of mission and ministry. This passage teaches us the communal nature of faith. When two or more people are gathered together, this eliminates the selfish intentions of prayer. In communal prayers, people pray for the community of faith and God's greater work for humanity.

Mission and Ministry

It is God's will that we be in mission work. Jesus said, "But you will receive power when the Holy Spirit comes on you; and you will be my witnesses in Jerusalem, and in all of Judea and Samaria, and to the ends of the earth." (Acts 1:8) Jesus said, "All authority in heaven and on earth has been given to me. Therefore go and make disciples of all nations, baptizing them in the name of the Father and of the Son and the Holy Spirit, and teaching them to obey everything I have commanded you." (Matthew 28:19-20) It is God's will that the church reach out to the world with the saving message of Jesus Christ. The church is to baptize and provide Christian education. As people live in the covenant of their baptisms, they grow in faith and the Christian life.

The church and Christian baptism are like a ship or ark that carries us over the tumultuous waters of life to the shores of salvation. The ship is unsinkable and will bring us eternal peace. The place of worship is often referred to as being the Nave. Nave is a Greek word meaning, "Boat." Navy comes from this word.

Vartov church, downtown Copenhagen, Denmark, has a model ship suspended from its ceiling. The ship represents the church that carries us over the waters of life to the shore of salvation. As the pastor of the church shared this message to a group of children, one of them asked, "If the church is unsinkable, then why are there lifeboats?" The pastor answered, "The lifeboats are for the members to go out to save and minister to the lost and hurting."

It is God's will that the church should reach out to the world that is hungry, homeless, and sick. The church is to show compassionate love in ministering to their needs. The church works to bring godly justice and peace to a world in need.

Three Keys

Here are three keys that will guide our prayers:

1) *Pray that God's will be done.*

2) *Pray that God will be glorified.*

3) *Pray in the name of Jesus.*

Pray that God's will be done.

We know that there are things that God wants us to pray for. Some examples of this would be: God wants us to be saved and give us eternal life. God desires to be in a relationship with us. God is eager to give us the Holy Spirit, so we can have fellowship with God. God wants us to live in obedience to his commandments. God has a purpose for us to love and serve others. God wants us to discern his will based on his Word. God calls us to share the good news of salvation with others. As we follow Jesus in these ways, we will be living a Christian life. God will answer our prayers and strengthen us in faith. We must pray for the will of God to be done, and he will provide for the purposes that he has called us to.

Pray that God will be glorified.

Jesus said, "Now is the Son of Man glorified and God is glorified in him. If God is glorified in him, God will glorify the Son in himself and will glorify him at once." (John 15:31-32) To glorify God is to give him the honor, respect, and credit. So many athletes give glory to God after they have won a championship. For these Christian athletes, they bring glory to God in their lives, whether they are playing in competition or being a Christian example in other areas of their lives. The motivation for all Christians is to give glory to God in their lives. We should not only pray that God's will be done, but we should also pray, "God be glorified in my life."

Pray in the name of Jesus.

Jesus said, "And I will do whatever you ask in my name, so that the Son may bring glory to the Father." (John 14:13) We pray in Jesus name because he is the authority. Jesus said, "All authority in heaven and earth has been given to me." (Matthew 28:18) We do not have the authority, but rather Jesus does. Jesus commands us to obey God's commandment in love, and bring salvation to the world by baptizing and instructing people to be his disciples.

Where does authority lie? Where do we seek permission? If I am at work, I will speak to my supervisor. If I were in the army, I would talk to my commander. As a Christian I pray to Jesus. Jesus is, "The way, the truth, and the life, no one comes to the Father but through him." (John 14:6) In all things we pray in the name of Jesus. Jesus' name is above all names, "At the name of Jesus every knee shall bow, in heaven and earth and under the earth, and every tongue confess that Jesus Christ is Lord." (Philippian 2:10-11) In all that we pray, we seek the authority of Jesus.

A follower of Jesus prays,

> "*Use me this day in whatever ways you see fit. Reveal to me your loving purpose for this day. God, I'm giving my life for your glory and work. Place the people along my path that you want me to love and serve this day. For life is not about me, but rather it is about you Lord. Use me as an instrument of your work.*" Amen.

It is God's will that we be in mission work ...It is God's will that the church should reach out to the world that is hungry, homeless, and sick.

QUESTIONS

1. Where is God's kingdom on earth?
2. What was God's will for Jesus?
3. Give an example of how God's will is sometimes the painful way?
4. God works good in all circumstances according to his will. What is God's good?
5. What is God's divine providence for humanity?
6. How do you feel the tension between praying, "My will be done" vs. "God's will be done?"
7. Why is praying for the greater needs of the community important?
8. How do you fit into God's purposes, rather than having God fit into ours?
9. How do you glorify God in your life?
10. Why is it important to pray in Jesus name?

Praying God's Word

The truth of God's Word, once you learn it, you will never forget it.

The Apostle Paul writes in Colossians 3:16-17, "Let the word of Christ dwell in you richly as you teach and admonish one another with all wisdom, and as you sing psalms, hymns and spiritual songs with gratitude in your hearts to God. And whatever you do, whether in word or deed, do it all in the name of the Lord Jesus, giving thanks to God the Father through him."

As we read our Bibles, fishing for God, we come to realize that it is God who hooks us. As we search for God, it is God who finds us. The Holy Spirit uses the Word to create the faith that clings to God.

It is important that we pray the Word. Jesus prayed the Word, when he was dying on the cross, he was quoting the Word, "My God, My God, why have you forsaken me?" (Psalm 22:1), and "Into your hands I commit my spirit." (Psalm 31:5)

We pray for the Holy Spirit to dwell in our hearts and minds, and the Holy Spirit uses the Word for building up Christian faith, "Consequently, faith comes from hearing the message, and the message is heard through the word of Christ." (Romans 10:17) "All Scripture is God-breathed and is useful for teaching, rebuking, correcting, and training in righteousness, so that the man of God may be thoroughly equipped for every good work." (2 Timothy 3:16-17) The Holy Spirit uses the Word of God to develop faith in the believers, and also for teaching, correcting, and training.

"For the word is living and active. Sharper than any double-edged sword." (Hebrews 4:12) The living Word of God is Jesus, he is the incarnate Son of God. The written Word of God is the Holy Bible. The Word of God was written by the Holy Spirit through human hands. Its central message is Jesus. As we read the Word of God, the Holy Spirit takes these words and makes them living in our lives. The Apostle Paul writes in Ephesians 6:17, "...the sword of the Spirit is the word of God." The sword has its two edges. The one edge of the sword is the moral law to convict us of our sins. The law of God is good, it sets the standard of God's expectations for our lives. As a fallen humanity, we fall short of this expectation. The other edge is the gospel, the good news of Jesus death and resurrection that brings forgiveness and new life. The Holy Spirit uses the Word to break down our old self with all of its sinful desires and raises up the new person of Jesus Christ.

The Word of God dwelt literally in Mary, as she was pregnant with Jesus. "My soul glorifies the Lord and my spirit rejoices in God my Savior." (Luke 1:46-47) As the Word of God dwells within us, we too are impregnated with the Word of Christ. Students who are studying to become pastors enroll in a seminary. The word seminary means, "To be inseminated with the Word of God."

Hearing

How do we get the Word of God within us? Jesus said, "He who has ears, let him hear." (Matthew 13:9) The Apostle Paul wrote, "Consequently, faith comes from hearing the message, and the message is heard through the word of Christ." (Romans 10:17) As we hear the Word of God, the Holy Spirit is convicting us of its message. We are internalizing the message of Jesus Christ within our hearts and minds.

Memorization.

Jesus said, "All that belongs to the Father is mine. That is why I said the Spirit will take from what is mine and make it known to you." (John 16:15) The Holy Spirit will bring back to remembrance all that Jesus has taught. The remembrance of all that Jesus has taught is recorded in the Gospels- Matthew, Mark, Luke, and John. As I stated above, the whole Bible is the final revelation of God. The Words of the Bible become living in us. As we memorize Bible verses and stories, the Holy Spirit etches them into our minds. Once we learn these verses, we will not forget them; the Holy Spirit will continue to bring them to our remembrance. When I was learning to ride a bike, at first it was a painful experience as I would crash my bike and skin my knees. Soon, riding a bike became second nature to me. My father said, "Once you learn how to ride a bike, you will never forget." The same was true with learning to type. My typing teacher said, "Once you learn how to type, this is a skill that you will never forget." The truth of God's Word, once you learn it, you will never forget it.

You start by memorizing verses, and those verses become living in you. I think of a verse like John 3:16 as a good one to start with. Psalm 23, is a good chapter to memorize. Just keep memorizing the Bible, and soon it will be incarnate in you. The Word will be living and active in your life. You will be able to apply the Word to all areas of your life.

Meditating on the Word of God.

"But his delight is in the law of the Lord, and on his law he meditates day and night." (Psalm 1:2) The law of God is also interpreted as the Word of God. We meditate on the Word of God, day and night.

Meditation is what we focus our minds on. It is like a stereo system, whatever CD we place in the tray is the music that it will play. If we place a CD of hard music, that is what the stereo plays, likewise if we put a CD with soft music. The Word is like a CD that we insert into our minds, God will be our focus. It is easy to meditate on negative things and people in our lives. This can give us a bad attitude toward life, and we can spend our energies worrying about so many unpleasant things. This is where we need to take the negative CD out of our minds, and replace it with a godly one.

We hear the Word of God, and then visualize the Word happening in our lives. We internalize the message by reflecting on what this Bible verse, story, or passage means for our lives.

We can hear the verse, John 3:16, "For God so loved the world, he gave his only begotten son, that whoever believes in him, will not perish but have eternal life." We meditate on this verse by visualizing God loving the world. Maybe we can visualize God giving the world a big hug. We look at God's loving arms as the cross that encompasses and holds the world. We can visualize the world hugging Jesus back. The pronoun, "Whoever" is like a computer chip that holds all the names of the world. It is a large pronoun. This pronoun also holds your name. We need to understand the love of God as being so personal, that if you were the only one living in this world, Jesus would have died for you! For God so loved [*your name*] that he gave his only son, that [*your name*] believes him will not perish, but have eternal life.

Another story is recorded in Mark 4:35-41, this is a story of Jesus being in a fishing boat with his disciples when a terrible storm arose. These experienced sailors were frightened for their lives. Jesus, who is fast asleep in the stern of the boat, is awaken and he calms the sea. As you hear this story, who or what do you relate to? What are your storms in life, whether they are literal or figurative storms? What frightens you about the storm? Even though you are experienced in life, when do you cry out to God in life? Why is Jesus asleep in the stern of the boat? Does Jesus know your peril? Does Jesus care? How have you experienced the storms subsiding, and you experience peace?

In verse 38, we read that Jesus was fast asleep on his pillow. Why is the pillow mentioned? We know the test of a restless spirit is when we cannot sleep. Jesus was at perfect peace; he could sleep on his pillow in the midst of the storm. Jesus gives us inner peace; we may sleep fast upon his pillow during the storms of life. "He who watches over you will not slumber." (Psalm 121:3)

In all Bible stories, you need to meditate on each verse, and ask, "How do I relate to this story? Who represents me in the story? How do I encounter God in life?

Modeled Prayers.

Sometimes we do not have the words to pray, so we pray modeled prayers. Jesus gave some modeled prayers. The most popular one would be "The Lord's Prayer." This prayer is all encompassing. Everything we need to be praying for is in this prayer. We pray to be in relationship with God, the Father. We honor God's name in this prayer. We pray for the kingdom of God to be established in our hearts. We pray that God's will be done. We pray that God will provide for our basic needs. We pray for forgiveness. We pray for strength against evil.

We can pray psalms as modeled prayers. There are psalms that are written as prayers for all occasions. Sometimes we do not have the words to pray, so we can pray a psalm. A psalm may have the words that fitly express what we are thinking and feeling. Psalm 8, is a psalm expressing our majestic wonder of God. Psalm 22, is a prayer of lament to God. Psalm 23, is a psalm of Jesus being our good shepherd. Psalm 46, is a prayer for protection during distressing times. Psalm 51, is a prayer of confession. Psalm 121, is a psalm of guidance, and then Psalms 144-150, are prayers of praise.

The Holy Spirit Prays For Us

"The Spirit himself testifies with our spirit that we are God's Children." (Romans 8:16) The Holy Spirit connects with our spirit, and the Holy Spirit who intercedes for us, prays on our behalf. The Holy Spirit is praying in and through the Christian believers lives. We cry out, "Father" as we live in fellowship with him. The Holy Spirit communicates God's presence in our lives. The Holy Spirit is evidence of God's resurrection life.

Amen

We generally conclude our prayers by saying, "Amen." Amen means, "So be it." In other words we agree with what has been prayed. This is our sincere heartfelt prayer to God. If we are in the company of other people praying, as we are engaged in listening to their prayers, when we agree with what is being prayed, then we pray, "Amen"; this person's prayer is also my prayer.

Just keep memorizing the Bible, and soon it will be incarnate in you. The Word will be living and active in your life. You will be able to apply the Word to all areas of your life.

QUESTIONS

1. Where is the Word of Christ to dwell?
2. Faith comes by what?
3. What are the two edges of God's Word?
4. How can we be impregnated with the Word of God?
5. Have you ever fished or searched for God?
6. What Bible verses have you memorized?
7. Why is it important to meditate on God's Word?
8. What modeled prayers have you used?
9. How does the Holy Spirit intercede for us?
10. How is God's Word living in you?

Prayer of Lament

As much as we don't like it,
suffering can strengthen us, if
we turn to God in prayer.

Nothing tests our faith more than human suffering. Suffering challenges our understanding of God. When we think of God as being a fairy godmother, a genie, or Santa Claus, our faith in these images gets tested. When we think that putting our faith in God will make us rich, healthy, and we will be now living a maintenance free life, suffering will challenge our faith. We begin to question whether or not there is even a God in times of trouble. At best we begin to think that God has caused all of my troubles - *God is a bully looking to inflict pain on me.* Another question that arises is, "Why didn't God prevent this horrible thing from happening?"

Reasons for Suffering

Here are reasons why people suffer:

1. *We are part of a fallen humanity.*

2. *We suffer by our own volition. It is hard for us to admit this; it is easier just to blame God or someone else.*

3. *We suffer because of someone else's actions.*

4. *We suffer as a result of natural disasters.*

5. *We suffer from illnesses and injury.*

6. *Sometimes there is no explanation for why we suffer. This was the case of the Biblical story of Job.*

Does God cause suffering? There are recorded instances in the Bible where God brought punishment to his people. This was disciplinary action. God's people were not worshiping and honoring him in life. The punishment was to bring people to repentance. When people say, "God has brought suffering upon me." I have to ask the question, "Is there something you need to repent of?" There are no Biblical stories or events of God bringing punishment upon people from sadistic motivations. When we worship God and obey his commandments, then God blesses us. When we fail to do this, then God does bring punishment. As we repent of our sins, God will be loving and gracious to forgive. We must remember, "For his anger lasts only a moment, but his favor lasts a lifetime." (Psalm 30:5)

The Grief Process

When bad things happen to us, we go through a grief process. Grief is a healing process we go through when we lose something. When a special person we love dies, we go through a grief process. When we lose a physical capacity, a job, or a possession that we value, we go through a grief process.

Some of the emotions of grief are shock, anger, sadness, and depression. As we allow ourselves to go through this process, we come to a place of healing. We know when we are healed when we can say, "I don't like what has happened. There will always be a sorrow, but life will go on in a good way." If we fail to grieve, life will not go on in a good way, and our grief will take the form of negativity, bitterness, and even abusiveness.

When suffering comes, if we have formed an image of God that is a house of cards, when the winds of adversity blow, our faith in God falls apart. Before Jesus' arrest, all of Jesus disciples betrayed him. They lost their faith in their God, and who Jesus was for them. They thought Jesus was going to be a strong governmental or military might, who would drive out the Romans, rather than a suffering servant who would die on a cross. Like the disciples, losing one's faith is a grief.

Strength in Weakness

As we live a prayerful life, God grants us wisdom to make good decisions that prevents much heartache from happening. God gives peace in the midst of trouble. God will often prevent bad things from happening. God will spare us from going through those awful times in life, but other times he will let us go through them. Adversity strengthens us. We will never grow strong if we do not go through times of struggle. As we pray during these times, God is with us. "God is our refuge and strength, a very present help in times of trouble." (Psalm 46:1) When we trust in God, he will make us stronger, wiser, and more compassionate.

The Apostle Paul wrote in 2 Corinthians 12:7-10, about a weakness he had. He referred to it as being a "Thorn in his flesh". He asked God repeatedly to remove this thorn, but Jesus said, "My grace is sufficient for you, for my power is made perfect in weakness." This weakness made him humble to always find his strength in God. His weakness became his strength, because God was his strength.

As we live a prayerful life, God grants us wisdom to make good decisions that prevents much heartache from happening.

I injured my leg many years ago playing football. This injury has made my leg weak. I prayed many times that God would heal it, but he never did. Instead, as I prayed, God was encouraging me, and strengthening me.

I have been able to run many marathons, including the Boston Marathon. God used my weakness to make me strong. If it hadn't been for that injury, I probably would have never set out to accomplish those running goals. God has used this chronic weakness to strengthen me in so many other ways as well. God can make our lives strong and productive even with chronic pain and illness.

When a runner runs against the wind, he becomes a stronger runner. When a swimmer swims against the current, she becomes a stronger swimmer. A butterfly's wings become strong to fly only as a result of wrestling to get out of its cocoon. As much as we don't like it, suffering can strengthen us, if we turn to God in prayer.

It is important in times of suffering not to judge and define God, ourselves, and life in a moment or event; but rather, over the course of time. We may not see God working in the moment. That is why we walk by faith. We trust that God is with us, and working in ways that we cannot ever imagine, to bring his strength. "For my thoughts are not your thoughts neither are your ways my ways." (Isaiah 55:8)

Jesus Brings Healing

"He himself bore our wounds you have been healed." (Isaiah 53:5; 1 Peter 2:24) It was from Jesus' deep wounds that God's healing comes for us. Some of the most compassionate and caring people that I know have gone through some of the most painful experiences in life. Some of the most hardened and bitter people that I know have gone through terrible times of suffering. The hot water that softens a bean is also the hot water that hardens an egg. Suffering and pain come to all people in various ways and levels. The questions that often get asked during these times are: "Why?" "How?" "What?" These questions are a progression as people work through the difficult times in their lives. We pray "Why?" when we do not understand. We pray "How?" as we wonder how God is going to help us. We pray "What?" as we use our suffering for the purposes of ministry.

Prayer of Why?

The prayer of "Why?" is the human cry to God when we are hurting. When we feel powerless in our pain, we do not know what to do, except crying out to God. Psalm 22:1, "My God, My God, why have you forsaken me?" These were the words that Jesus cried from the cross, as he was suffering in excruciating pain. As we read the entire Psalm 22, it describes vividly a person who is suffering on a cross. This psalm was prophetic, written a thousand years before Jesus death.

God gives peace in the midst of trouble. God will often prevent bad things from happening ... but other times he will let us go through them.

The prayer of "Why?" is an honest prayer. We are praying a real emotion of anger to God. In these moments we need a cathartic release, and a good way of doing that is praying our anger to God. When we are honest before God then we can begin the healing process. The prayer of "Why?" is a lack of understanding. This circumstance makes no sense. It defies all common reasoning and logic, it is unjust, and I have lost all power and control over the situation.

Adversity strengthens us. We will never grow strong if we do not go through times of struggle... when we trust in God, he will make us stronger, wiser, and more compassionate.

We are part of a fallen humanity. As we read the story of the fall in Genesis 3:1-7, the devil tempted Adam and Eve to eat the forbidden fruit. He placed the forbidden tree in the Garden as a choice for them to make. God created Adam and Eve (Humanity) to be in relationship with him, but God wants that relationship to be based on a mutual love. God does not want a relationship based on control, manipulation, or coercion any more than any of us. God doesn't want to be a controlling puppeteer. When loving someone, there is the risk that the person will not reciprocate that love. That was the loving risk that God needed to take.

The Devil gave the temptation that they would be God if they ate the fruit. This was humanity's fall from God. Humanity chose to live as one's own god, rather than to live in the loving relationship with God, the Father. The first commandment ultimately is: "Do not be God!"

The original sin of humanity is to be God. The attitude of humanity before God is one of saying, "I am god! I don't need anyone, including God to tell me what to do!" We claim to be autonomous, knowing what is right and good for us.

The second attitude is judgment. Humanity now knows what is best for the world and others, so we will try to exercise power over others. We will also be critical of others when they have shown less than perfection according to our personal standards that we would have for them. Humanity now sets itself on the judgment seat to condemn the moral ideals and actions of others, but also self-justifies through what humanity defines as being the good standard of the moral good.

The third attitude is one of contention. This attitude shows greed, dominance, and is willing to show violent force to exercise its will.

The fourth attitude is one of blame. Humanity made the choice to separate from God, but yet when something bad happens, the blame is placed on God.

Even though we messed-up, in our twisted thinking, we blame God for it. God did not eat the forbidden fruit, humanity did! This blame turns to anger. We become bitter toward God, and finally that leads to cursing God. Humanity's sinful condition views itself as perfect and God has messed-up. In actuality, sin has brought consequences, suffering, and death.

All of these attitudes are also societal. We suffer not only as individuals, but also as a society. The community suffers and asks the question "Why?" The community cries: Why war? Why racism? Why injustice? Why oppression? Why greed? Society as a whole suffers the consequences of systemic sin.

The Prayer of How?

The question of "Why", becomes a question of "How"? How does God help in times of trouble? God helps us by showing his mercy. "I will have mercy on whom I have mercy, and I will have compassion on whom I have compassion." (Romans 9:15) God shows his mercy by sending Jesus to die on a cross for us. God loves all people, but how does he love us? "But God demonstrates his own love for us in this; while we were still sinners, Christ died for us." (Romans 5:8) God's love and mercy are shown to all people through the cross of Jesus. The one side of the cross stands for injustice, pain, trouble, sin, and death; while the other side of the cross represents resurrection, forgiveness, healing and life. It is by Jesus wounds that we are healed.

In the midst of our suffering, where is God? God is on the cross, taking on the pain, suffering, and all the things that don't make sense about our broken world. God is working through the church. When the World Trade Center was attacked on September 11, 2001, people asked where is God in the midst of this evil event? There were two steel girders that formed a cross in the midst of the debris. That became the focal point of rescuers and mourners. The cross always stands before us in the midst of life and tragedy. It is at the cross where God meets humanity. The cross stands as the truth of our fallen humanity, and the truth of God's love and sacrifice. It is out of the ashes of death, that new life comes. "This is what the Sovereign Lord says to these bones: I will make breath enter you, and you will come to life." (Ezekiel 37:5) Job said, "I know that my Redeemer lives, and that in the end he will stand upon the earth. And after my skin has been destroyed, yet in my flesh I will see God." (Job 19:26-26) God brings resurrection and new life, out of suffering and death. Jesus Christ who suffered and died on the cross is risen from the dead. We pray that the resurrection life of Jesus, we bring new life for us in the midst of tragedy.

The church is to carry the cross of Jesus. We enter into the dark valleys of life, and we bring the healing and hope of Jesus. As a church, we work to carry each other's burdens. Mark 2:1-12, is recorded the story of four men carrying their paralytic friend to Jesus. They recognized that Jesus could heal their friend. The church is a friend of people. We gather to provide resources for people in times of trouble. Many hands make for light work. So many people can carry us through the difficult times of life. God is working through the vocations of compassionate people. Cross-bearing Christians are not concerned about God providing a life of wealth and pleasure for us, but rather having God inspire us to be self-sacrificing people who are looking to give our lives away for the sake of God and others. Jesus said, "If anyone would come after me, he must deny himself and take up his cross and follow me. For whoever wants to save his life will lose it, but whoever loses his life for me will find it." (Matthew 16:24-25)

God has given us the stewardship of caring, healing, and binding up the broken. God brings healing and peace to our lives. "The Spirit of the Sovereign Lord is on me, because the Lord has anointed me to preach good news to the poor. He has sent me to bind up the brokenhearted, to proclaim freedom for the captives and release from darkness from the prisoners." (Isaiah 61:1)

The church is the loving presence of Jesus in the world, working to alleviate human suffering of war, of hunger, of greed, of injustice, of racism, of oppression, and of sickness. The church is praying, and God is empowering the church to action. The church is the body of Christ, being the hands, the feet, the eyes, the ears, and the mouth of God's loving compassion. One of the fallacies of religion is, "God will not give you more than you can handle." This is a reference to 1 Corinthians 10:13. This is Paul addressing temptation. As far as pain and suffering, people do bear more than what they can handle, and that is one reason why God has given us the church, so that we can bear one another's burdens.

It is important in times of suffering not to judge and define God, ourselves, and life in a moment or event; but rather, over the course of time. We may not see God working in the moment.

Three things that we must ascertain as we face distressful situations. We must remember that, "God is our refuge and strength, a very present help in times of trouble." (Psalm 46:10) With this in mind we always:

1) *Identify the problem.*

2) *Understand what options we have in confronting the problem.*

3) *Know, when choosing an option, what resources we have in exercising the option.*

When we live for the purposes of God, God uses all the circumstances of our lives to bring forth his goodness. King David wrote, "Even though I walk through the valley of the shadow of death, I will fear no evil, for you are with me, your rod and your staff, they comfort me." (Psalm 23:4) God goes with us to the deepest and darkest valleys of our lives. It is even at these times, the light of Jesus shines.

What Does God Plan?

Even though it was not God's will and plan for humanity to fall to sin, God works his redemptive salvation in our lives. God took the most horrific historical event, the crucifixion of Jesus, and has brought forth the greatest moment in the world's history, the resurrection of Jesus from the dead. Humanity meant evil in crucifying Jesus, but God has used it for good. God is always bringing new life to us, "Therefore, if anyone is in Christ, he is a new creation; the old has gone, the new has come!" (2 Corinthians 5:17) God does this because of his amazing love and grace for us. We pray that God is working in the suffering of our world to bring healing and peace.

Cross-bearing Christians are not concerned about God providing a life of wealth and pleasure for us, but rather having God inspire us to be self-sacrificing people

What is God doing through our time of suffering? He is building us up, "...suffering produces perseverance; perseverance, character; and character, hope." (Romans 5:3-4) God gives us three strengths during times of suffering. When God gives us perseverance, we can endure times of suffering. A godly attitude will help us have a right perspective on things. When we have hope, we have reason to continue in life. God builds up Christian character, and that is strength for life.

When Jesus healed the leper, he said, "Your faith has made you well." (Luke 17:19) It wasn't the healing that made him well; it was his faith that made him well. Faith in Jesus makes us complete before God. Jesus precious blood is the complete reconciliation for our sins before God. When people come to faith, it is like putting gasoline on a pilot flame. The person ignites with a passion for God. They are able to use the pains of their difficult life situations and show compassionate love toward others. I have known people with spinal cord injuries, who now minister encouragement to others who have experienced similar injuries. I have known people who have suffered deep grief, but now minister comfort to others who are grieving. I have known people who are recovering from addictions, who are now ministering to others who struggle with addictions. The Apostle Paul wrote, "Praise be to the God and Father of our Lord Jesus Christ, the Father of compassion and the God of all comfort, who comforts us in all our troubles, so that we can comfort those in any trouble with the comfort we ourselves have received from God." (2 Corinthians 1:3-4)

"Then I saw a new heaven and a new earth, for

the first heaven and the first earth had passed away, and there was no longer any sea. I saw the Holy City, the new Jerusalem, coming down out of heaven from God, prepared as a bride beautifully dressed for her husband. And I heard a loud voice from the throne saying 'Now the dwelling of God is with men, and he will live with them. They will be his people, and God himself will be with them and be their God. He will wipe every tear from their eyes. There will be no more death or mourning or crying or pain, for the old order of things has passed away.'" (Revelation 21:1-4) John received this vision of the church on earth, as it is in heaven. In heaven, there will be no death, no suffering, no mourning, no greed, no injustice, no racism, and no hunger. God's vision for his church on earth is a heavenly one. Just as we will dwell with God in heaven, God wants to dwell with us on this earth. The church must continue to pray for this vision to be our world's reality.

The trials of life will always reveal our true attitudes and character ... When we pray, the Holy Spirit is forging a character that will withstand the tests of life.

Turning Negatives into Positives

Negative or bad things happen in life. This is inevitable. The question is, "What do we do with it?" We can use the bad things that happen in life, and develop a bitter attitude toward God and others. Negative energy is energy, and we can use it for destructive ends. The alternative is taking this energy and using it for constructive purposes. Jesus took the negative energy of the cross to build up his church on earth.

In my personal life, I have used negative energy to fuel my marathon running or for ministry projects. It is important to take the negative energy of bad things that have happened and channel it into positive/godly purposes.

St. Peter writes, "These have come so that your faith-of greater worth than gold, which perishes even though refined by fire-may be proved genuine and may result in praise, glory and honor when Jesus Christ is revealed." (1 Peter 1:7) Fire can either consume or it will refine. Peter refers to our faith as being more precious than gold. God can use those difficult times in our lives, so that our faith being tested by fire will not be consumed, but rather refined to the praise, glory and honor of God.

The trials of life will always reveal our true attitudes and character. Our whole person will be challenged. When we pray, the Holy Spirit is forging a character that will withstand the tests of life.

The prayer of lament is cathartic. Four things about a prayer of lament:

1) *We vent our negative emotions to God.*

2) *We remember God's goodness in our lives. Jesus died for us.*

3) *We receive the joy of God's presence in the Holy Spirit.*

4) *We worship God in thanksgiving and praise for all his goodness. The Lament Psalms have this form of movement.*

QUESTIONS

1. When did you experience a major trial in life?
2. What emotions did you experience with the trials?
3. How do trials make you bitter or make you stronger?
4. Explain your prayer of why?
5. What are the attitudes of original sin?
6. Explain your prayer of how?
7. What did God plan in your trial?
8. What three strengths does God give us in suffering?
9. What vision does God give to the world?
10. How can you take negative energy and use it for something positive?

Prayer of Confession

> *Prayers of confession bring us to a place of pardon and peace in our lives. We can walk with our heads lifted with confidence.*

Confession is to admit our guilt. This is not the easiest thing to do, because we want to make the case of being a good person before God. We want to make our case for righteousness. We don't want to have the feeling of falling short of the glory of God, but rather, that God is pleased with us. Sin is doing what is wrong. Sin is breaking God's good law, and being disobedient to his sovereign will for our lives and society.

How Do We Know That We Have Sinned?
The law of God reveals our sins. The law of God is recorded in the first five books of the Bible known as the Pentateuch. Most specifically the law would be the Ten Commandments recorded in Exodus 20:1-17. The

law of God is good. It creates order for society and the standard that God wants us to live by. Sin has weakened us, to where we fall short of the laws expectations. The Apostle Paul wrote, "I would not have known what sin was except through the law. For I would not have known what coveting really was if the law had not said, 'Do not covet.'" (Romans 7:7)

A second way that we know that we have sinned is through our conscience. God has given us a conscience to know right from wrong. God spoke through the prophet Jeremiah saying, "I will put my law in their minds and write it on their hearts." (Jeremiah 31:33)

A third way that we know that we have sinned is through the loving concern of Christian believers for whom we are held accountable. "If your brother sins against you, go and show him his fault, just between the two of you." (Matthew 18:15)

It is hard to admit our sins because it is embarrassing, there are consequences to our sins, and we lose our repute. We learn at a young age that if we just lie, deny, or make an excuse for our sinfulness, we can get out of trouble.

We may lie about our sins. Often times, we have to make up more lies to cover-up the one lie. Life becomes complicated as we try to remember all the lies to cover-up our sins. I knew an elderly man who had lost his short-term memory. Someone asked him, "Why are you so honest?" He replied, "I cannot remember what I said the day before, so I better be telling the truth." Lying does not take away the guilt of sin, nor does it repair its damages.

How do we know when someone is lying? There is a lie detector test that we need to be aware of. Here are three things that will let us know that someone is lying: The first is facial expressions. No matter how hard we try to have a poker face, our face will show our guilt. The second indicator is when someone says, "I swear by God", or "I swear on a stack of Bibles." Whenever someone says this, they are admitting their guilt. The third indication is when someone's story changes. When a person is telling the truth, he knows the truthful story, so it will never change no matter how many times he tells it, but when a person is lying the story will change.

We may lie about our sins ... Lying does not take away the guilt of sin, nor does it repair its damages.

We can deny our sins. This is when a person fights against the truth. The truth is like a mirror that we cannot deny, but yet we may give it our best effort. As a youth, I remember camping with friends outside of my hometown. One of my friends wanted to bring payback to his friend who wronged him, so in the middle of the night we went to his friend's house. He climbed through the garage window, and let the air out of his friend's bike tires. My other friends waited with me in a cornfield by his house. We didn't know what was taking him so long. Finally he came out, we hiked back to our camp, and went to sleep. The next morning when I got home, my mother was waiting for me, and asked, "What were you doing at the Smith's house last night?" I said, "I wasn't at the Smith's house!" She said again, "What were you doing at the Smith's house last night?" I said, "I wasn't at the Smith's house!" A third time my mother asked, "What were you doing at the Smith's house?" I realized my mother did not believe my denial, so I had to admit my guilt. She said, "Someone let all the air out of their tires, including the car tires. Mr. Smith was not able to make it to work." That explained why it took my friend so long in the garage.

Sometimes people can be in such denial of telling the truth, they will hire a lawyer to get them off the hook. The lawyer cannot take away the guilt or the damage of the sin.

We can make excuses for our sins. We can admit our sins, but blame others for it. I think of God confronting Adam after he ate the forbidden fruit. Adam blamed Eve for tempting him, so it was Eve's fault that he sinned. Eve blamed the serpent, and the serpent could blame the Devil. The Devil is the origin of sin and evil, but still we have to take responsibility for our wrong doings.

When we lie, deny, and make excuses for our sins, we are covering things up. We are hiding our sins, just as Adam and Eve tried to hide their sins with fig leaves. We try to place everything in the dark where others cannot see them. Even though we may do a masterful job of covering up our sins from other people, we must remember that we cannot hide things from God. God knows the very depth of our hearts. Psalm 139:1 reads, "O Lord, you have searched me and you know me." God is light, and he will expose our sins. When we cover-up our sins, it is still there and it weighs down our souls. We have a guilty conscience. The guilt takes away all the joy of life.

Jesus Pays the Price

When we sin, someone else pays the price for our actions. If we steal from someone, they suffer the loss. There are always consequences to sin. If we get caught stealing, then we suffer the consequences. Whether we get caught sinning or not, we will always suffer the consequences of it.

The debt of our sin is beyond what we can pay. As we read in Romans 5:8, it is Jesus who pays the price for our sins, "But God demonstrates his own love for us in this: While we were still sinners, Christ died for us." Jesus, who knew no sin, suffered and died in our place. Just as God provided a sacrifice for Isaac (Genesis 22:13), and a Passover Lamb for his people in Egypt (Exodus 12:5-7), God has provided a sacrifice for us. The sacrifices needed to be without spot or blemish (Leviticus 1:2) Jesus has to be without sin, to take away our sins. He is the perfect Lamb of God to take away the sins of the world. (1 Peter 2:19) Jesus is God in human flesh. Only God is without sin; Jesus is nothing less than God. One sinner dying for another sinner does not negate sin. In that moment of Jesus death on the cross, Jesus is the expiation of all humanity's sins: past, present, and future.

As God's people, our faith wavers. One day, we may feel strong in faith, while the next we may feel weak.

As we read in Romans 6:3-4, the Apostle Paul writes, "Or don't you know that all of us who were baptized into Christ Jesus were baptized into his death. We were therefore buried with him through baptism into death in order that, just as Christ was raised from the dead through the glory of the Father, we too might live a new life." We receive the salvation of God in our baptisms. When we are baptized, we are united with Jesus in his death and resurrection. God establishes a relationship with him. We enter into God's house, as we are reborn his children. As we live in this covenantal relationship, God is always faithful. His Word of promise is one that remains forever. As God's people, our faith wavers. One day, we may feel strong in faith, while the next we may feel weak. We do not put our faith in ourselves, but rather in what God has promised. As a parent and child walk across the street, it is the parent's grip that will get the child across the street, and not the other way around. It is God's never-ending grip that we cling to. We renew the covenant of our baptisms daily through confession and forgiveness. Daily, we drown out the old sinful self through confession that the new person in Christ may rise up through forgiveness.

When we confess our sins, God will forgive us our sins, and we will have peace with him and with each other. We are justified. Justification means, "To be declared not guilty." We are justified through the death and resurrection of Jesus. We receive his forgiveness. "Therefore, since, we have been justified through faith, we have peace with God through our Lord Jesus Christ, through whom we have gained access by faith into this grace in which we now stand." (Romans 5:1-2)

With confession there is also repentance. Repentance is not only confessing our sins, but it is also changing our sinful behavior. It is turning from sin . . .

Justification is a legal term. It is a declaration of being absolved from our sins. A lawyer will be an advocate standing before the judge, hoping for a "Not guilty" verdict. As we read in 1 John 2:1, we have an advocate who speaks on our behalf. He is the one who dies for us, and presents us before God as one who no longer is seen as a sinner, but rather as one who is redeemed; "But if anybody does sin, we have one who speaks to the Father on our defense-Jesus Christ, the Righteous One." Jesus is like a lawyer who presents us before God, declaring us justified.

As we read in 1 John 1:9, we hear the promise of Jesus, "If we confess our sins, he is faithful and just and will forgive us our sins and purify us from all unrighteousness." It is better to have God take the weight of our sin away, rather than have our conscience burdened down. When we are forgiven we are free, and our righteousness has been restored. Jesus said, "If you hold to my teaching, you are really my disciples. Then you will know the truth, and truth will set you free." (John 8:31-32)

Confessions and Absolutions

David was arguably the greatest king in Israel's history, but even he had his downfall. "One evening David got up from his bed and walked around on the roof of the palace. From the roof he saw a woman bathing. The woman was very beautiful and David sent someone to find out about her. The man said, 'Isn't this Bathsheba, the daughter of Eliam and the wife of Uriah the Hittite?' Then David sent messengers to get her. She came to him, and he slept with her. (She had purified herself from her uncleanness.) Then she went back home. The woman conceived and sent word to David, saying, 'I'm pregnant.'" (2 Samuel 11:2-5) "In the morning David wrote a letter to Joab and sent it with Uriah. In it he wrote, 'Put Uriah in the front line where the fighting is fiercest. Then withdraw from him so he will be struck down, and die.'" (2 Samuel 11:14-15) King David broke all of the commandments. He coveted his neighbor's wife, he committed adultery, he saw to it that Uriah was killed in battle, he bore false witness by covering up his actions, he dishonored his parent's, he stole his neighbor's wife, and he dishonored God. David thought he had gotten away with all of this. God would not allow him to get away with breaking all of his commandments, and that is the thing we must all realize. Ultimately God is our judge, and he is just. The day of reckoning comes to all people. God has his ways of going about justice. How could God get David to repent? God called on the prophet Nathan to confront David. How could Nathan go before the King who has just covered up his scandal without getting his head chopped off? Nathan's approach was to have David reveal his guilt for himself. Nathan tells the story of a man who had everything, and another man who only had one little ewe lamb. The wealthy man was so greedy that he stole the little ewe lamb from the other man. Nathan asked David, "What do you think of this man?" David was incensed and felt the man should be put to death. Nathan said to David, "You are the man!" (2 Samuel 12:7) King David was exposed, but yet God forgave him when he made confession.

Psalm 51 is King David's confession. I will highlight some of the verses:

Verse 1, "Have mercy on me, O God, according to your unfailing love; according to your great compassion blot out my transgressions." King David no longer was denying and covering up his wrongful actions, but rather is confessing them before God. He is begging for God's mercy. We also must confess our sins and beg God's mercy.

Verse 7, "Cleanse me with hyssop, and I will be clean; wash me, and I will be whiter than snow." It is only God who can cleanse us from our sins. It is by the blood of Jesus that we are made clean.

Verse10, "Create in me a pure heart, O God, and renew a steadfast spirit within me." When we are cleansed of our sin, we need to replace it with the indwelling of the Holy Spirit. Our heart has been cleansed, and now the holiness of God dwells within us by the Holy Spirit.

Verse 13, "Then I will teach transgressors your ways, and sinners will turn back to you." One of the best ways to be a recovering sinner is to help and teach others the ways of God.

Verse 15, "O Lord, open my lips and my mouth will declare your praise." God transforms us to be people of praise. He releases us from the bondage of sin, and allows us to be people of honor, glory, and praise to him.

Verse 19, "Then there will be righteous sacrifices whole burnt offerings to delight you; then bulls will be offered on your altar." As the Apostle Paul writes in Romans 12:1, "Therefore, I urge you, brothers, in view of God's mercy, to offer your bodies as living sacrifices, holy and pleasing to God-this is your spiritual act of worship." The offering that we are to give to God is ourselves'. We live our lives to the service of God's glory.

Peter was a close disciple to Jesus. He loved Jesus and even said he would die for him. Jesus said to Peter, "Before the rooster crows, you will deny me three times." This did happen after Jesus was arrested. In John 21:15-19, Jesus meets up with his disciples on the Sea of Galilee following the resurrection. Three times Jesus asks Peter, "Do you love me?" Peter each time responded by saying, "Yes, I love you." This was a threefold confession. Peter was forgiven, and was freed to follow the risen Jesus as one of his apostles'.

When we have a grievance with another person, we can feel the tension that exists. This is what sin does to our relationship with God, it brings a tension, wondering; does God love me? Should I come into his presence for worship? Am I condemned to hell? Just as Jesus cleared the tension with Peter by forgiving him, so God wants to make everything right with us. God wants us all to have the confidence that we are his children. We are his children for whom he is pleased.

I knew a youth who was humorous, friendly, and for whom I enjoyed as his pastor. He came from a broken home and had some personal struggles. One day he came to me and said, "I'm moving away to live with my father. You won't forget me pastor?" I said, "No, I won't forget you." Some time had elapsed when I got a phone call from his aunt; she was frantic saying, "He had been shot in the head!" Apparently it was a drug deal that had gone bad. He was shot in the head. The gunshot should have killed him instantly; instead he was healed from his wound, but leaving him with loss of sight.

He came to my office one night with a friend and

said, "I need to make confession because I have broken everyone of God's commandments." I heard his confession and pronounced forgiveness.

He then went to a school for the blind where he would learn how to read brail. It wasn't too long after he left that his aunt called me all frantic again saying, "He had been killed in a car accident." I believe that it was God's divine providence that spared his life from the gunshot wound. He should have died, but he was not ready to meet God. He had to make things right before meeting his judge. On the day he died, I know that he was ready to meet God who will judge him not guilty. It is through confession and forgiveness that we are made righteous in God's sight. God no longer sees us as sinners, but rather as clothed in the righteousness of Jesus.

Sins of Commission and Omission

We confess our sins of commission and also our sins of omission. The **sins of commission** are the sins that we commit. Some of these sins we are very aware of, while others we may not realize. We can do the things that hurt others and bring grief to God. Many times, we are not even aware of them.

The **sins of omission** are the right things that we have failed to do in life. It is one thing to do things that are wrong, but it is another to fail to do the things that are right. We can sit in a room and stare at a wall all day; we can say at the end of the day, "I have not committed any sin." What is sinful, we have failed to do anything productive in loving our neighbors and serving those in need.

Sin has its consequences. We suffer these consequences in our lives. Even though King David was forgiven, there were consequences to his actions. The son who was born to him, died.

With confession there is also repentance. Repentance is not only confessing our sins, but it is also changing our sinful behavior. It is turning from sin, death, and the Devil, and living by the Holy Spirit. When we repent of our sins, we receive the rebirth of a new life. Eternal life begins at this rebirth. We do not have to wait until we die to have eternal life with God. It begins at our baptisms, as we are reborn as children of God. For those who are in Jesus, death now is a transition from life on earth, to life in heaven.

As stated above, the consequences of sin is death. If we do not repent, this sin leads to a second death, and that it eternal condemnation in hell. "Then death and Hades were thrown into the lake of fire. The lake of fire is the second death." (Revelation 20:14) "Whoever believes in him is not condemned, but whoever does not believe stands condemned already because he has not believed in the name of God's one and only Son." (John 3:18)

The Apostle Paul writes, "Therefore, there is now no condemnation for those who are in Christ Jesus, because through Christ Jesus the law of the Spirit of life set me free from the law of sin and death." (Romans 8:1)

We confess our sins and hear the words of absolution, but still there are some sins that trouble our conscience even after we have confessed them. We may think that they are the unforgiveable sins. In these times, it is good to meet with a confessor who can not only pronounce forgiveness, but also give spiritual counsel to work through the agitated spirit. God wants us to be at peace with him, and also with one another.

As we confess our sins and receive forgiveness, it is also important to do an assessment of those good values and traits that we possess. It is upon this goodness that we can build our lives into the spiritual temple that God wants us to be. It is using the gifts, talents, and good character traits that we can use to serve and honor God with our lives. God is always working to transform and develop us into mature people of Jesus Christ. The Apostle Paul wrote, "Not that I have already obtained all this, or have already been made perfect, but I press on to take hold of that for which Christ Jesus took hold of me." (Philippians 3:12)

As we confess our sins and receive forgiveness, it is also important to do an assessment of those good values and traits that we possess.

As a Bible camp counselor, I gave a little piece of paper to each camper. They were to write on the paper their sins and then we nailed the pieces of paper to a wooden cross. I then lit the pieces of paper on fire, and we watched them burn, until I blew the fire out. What remained on the cross were the charred pieces of paper that looked like a black rose. It is from the cross that we confess our sins, are forgiven, and see the beauty of living in the love and grace of God. "If we confess our sins, he is faithful and just and will forgive us our sins and purify us from all unrighteousness." (1 John 1:9) This is God's loving promise!

Prayers of confession bring us to a place of pardon and peace in our lives. We can walk with our heads lifted with confidence. God has given us a clear conscience.

QUESTIONS

1. What is confession?
2. How do we know we have sinned?
3. Why is it hard to admit sin?
4. What are ways that we cover-up sins?
5. Who pays the price for our sins?
6. What does justification mean?
7. Who were Bible people who confessed their sins?
8. What are sins of commission?
9. What are sins of omission?
10. What is God's promise of confession?

Prayer of Praise

A prayer of praise is one where we direct our adoration and glory to God. We experience the joy of worship.

"And they were calling to one another: 'Holy, holy, holy is the Lord Almighty; the whole earth is full of his glory.'" (Isaiah 6:3) The glory of the God filled the temple, and the angels gathered to worship.

"Hallelujah! For our Lord God Almighty reigns. Let us rejoice and be glad and give him glory!" (Revelation 19:6-7) God's holy people gather around the throne of God's glory, receiving the salvation that he so graciously gives, and to give our lives to God, as we worship his holy name.

God loves our praise! God has created us for praise! We praise God in worship. We are created in God's image, so we enjoy praise. When someone praises us, this is a sign of their love and affection for us; it reinforces the good behaviors that we have shown to others.

We may go to a music concert or an athletic event where the large crowds of people are praising those who are performing. We are expressing our excitement for what we are experiencing. Many times we can praise athletes and music makers, but our worship has no expression. We need to praise God the same way we would if we went to a concert or athletic event. God wants our praise above all other things!

We may praise God for all the good things he has done, but the main thing is to praise God for who he is. We don't praise our children so much because they have made good grades or have had athletic accomplishments; we praise them because they are our children. We praise God for being our loving Heavenly Father.

We praise with our singing, our clapping, and our playing musical instruments. All of creation praises God. To hear the sound of crashing ocean waves, the wind blowing through the trees, and the birds singing, are delightful melodies. I enjoy camping alongside a river. At night as I lay in my tent, I can hear all the sounds of nature. The sounds of insects, frogs, and rushing water are an orchestra of praise to God.

Psalm 150 is a psalm of praise to God:
> *"Praise the Lord.*
> *Praise God in his sanctuary;*
> *Praise him in his mighty heavens;*
> *Praise him for his acts of power;*

Praise him for his surpassing greatness.
Praise him with the sounding of the trumpet
Praise him with the harp and the lyre,
Praise him with tambourine and dancing,
Praise him with the strings and the flute,
Praise him with the clash of cymbals,
Praise him with resounding cymbals.
Let everything that has breath praise the Lord
Praise the Lord."

We join together with all of creation, praising God. The Apostle Paul writes, "Praise be to the God and Father of our Lord Jesus Christ, who has blessed us in the heavenly realms with every spiritual blessing in Christ....to bring all things in heaven and on earth together under one head, even Christ." (Ephesians 1:3,10)

We praise God for who he is, but we also praise God for creating all things. As we live in the life support system of creation, we thank God for it. We thank God for the air, food, shelter, and water; but we also thank God for the beauty of it. To see the oceans, the mountains, the sunrises and the sunsets, we praise God. For all of creation is a reflection of his handiwork.

We thank God for giving to us Jesus, who is our savior. Jesus has given us eternal life, and has united all things in heaven and on earth. God has blessed humanity with creation and all the spiritual blessings of heaven.

When Jesus was born, the angels rejoiced, "Glory to God in the highest, and on earth peace to men on whom his favor rests." (Luke 2:14) When you were brought to salvation, the angels rejoiced! (Luke 15:10)

Praise is the exhilaration of our innermost person, our soul. It is out of the depth of our hearts and minds that we praise God. It is only God who can reach into the very depth of our soul, and allow his transforming power to take affect in our lives. The Apostle Paul writes in Romans 8:15-16, "For you did not receive a spirit that makes you a slave again to fear, but you received the Spirit of sonship. And by him we cry, 'Abba, Father,' The Spirit himself testifies with our spirit that we are God's children." Praise is the expression of joy that is placed in the innermost part of our being by the Holy Spirit. The Holy Spirit gives us the joy of his salvation. We praise God for being his children. We are no longer slaves, enemies, or sinners before God, but rather the redeemed children of God!

So many of the great hymns of the church are ageless sermons.

An anthem is a spiritual song based on Bible verses. It is God's Word that becomes the song of our lives. The Holy Spirit uses the Word to inspire us. As we read in Colossians 3:16, "Let the word of Christ dwell in you richly as you teach and admonish one another with all wisdom, and as you sing psalms, hymns and spiritual songs with gratitude in your hearts to God." It is our hearts desire that the Word of God will dwell in our hearts richly; that the Word becomes living and active in our lives. Music has a way of doing that. Music has a way of entering into the very depth of our hearts and minds. When we put music to the Word, we can memorize it. As Bible camp counselors, we would teach youth Bible verses by putting music to them.

So many of the great hymns of the church are ageless sermons. As a pastor of the church, if my sermon isn't reaching anyone, hopefully the profound message of the hymns will enter into the hearts and minds of people.

Martin Luther was a hymn writer, as was Charles Wesley who wrote over 6,000 hymns. Many of these hymns are printed in our church song books today. Chris Tomlin, and Michael W. Smith are contemporary songwriters. Has God put a song in your heart? We can sing the great traditional hymns, such as, "**How Great Thou Art**", and "**Amazing Grace**". We can also sing some of the more contemporary songs such as, "**I can only Imagine**," and "**How Great is Our God.**"

A Life of Praise

"Let the word of Christ dwell in you richly as you teach and admonish one another with all wisdom, and as you sing psalms, hymns and spiritual songs with gratitude in your hearts to God." (Colossians 3:16)

I was going to a Christian television station to be interviewed. As I got to the door, it sounded like heaven on the other side. People were singing and praising God.

As I went in, it was the staff of the Christian station. They were gathered around a piano, singing praises to God. Finally, someone said, "We need to get to work, so they were quoting Bible verses with each other, as they were getting ready to record my interview. After the interview, they gathered around the piano and started singing more praise songs to God. Praise is their lifestyle.

Having a song or melody in our heart uplifts our spirit. We can express our praise to God wherever we are, or whatever circumstances we are having. I know a lady who shares a childhood memory of her father working in his fields. She could hear him on his tractor singing his favorite hymns. When we have a spiritual song in our hearts, the Devil has no place to plant his feet.

I once was trying to promote a new hymnal to the congregation that I was serving. A member said, "Does the new hymnal have The Old Rugged Cross?" I said, "I'm sure that it does, it has all the good old favorite hymns, plus some of the favorite contemporary songs." He said, "If it has the Old Rugged Cross, I will be a big contributor in buying the new hymnals." After the worship service, I went to my office and perused the sample copy. I looked for the Old Rugged Cross and I couldn't find it. When the man came to my office, I looked dejected as I said, "It doesn't have the Old Rugged Cross." The man said, "I'll take an old hymnal, and I'll bring it to a printer where we can have copies made that can be pasted in the back of the new hymnals." Because of this man's efforts, our church has hymnals with the Old Rugged Cross. This hymn is his anthem for life. The Old Rugged Cross has a melody that he likes, but more importantly a sermon having a lifelong message.

> *"This is my story, this is my song,*
> *praising my Savior all the day long."*
> **– Blessed Assurance**

Having a song or melody in our heart uplifts our spirit ... When we have a spiritual song in our hearts, the Devil has no place to plant his feet.

The Power of Praise

Praise brings down the walls of sin, death, and the Devil. In Joshua 6, we hear the story of God's army under the direction of Joshua attacking Jericho. This was the first battle of many in conquering the Promised Land. Cities had large walls of defense around them. God gave them the plan of attack. They did not wage war with swords, battering rams, and catapults, but rather the praises of God. For seven days they were to march around the city, blowing their trumpets, and on the seventh day, with a large shout the walls came tumbling down. It was by the victorious praises of God's people that Jericho was defeated that day. As Christian people we praise God, and sing, "Jesus Christ is Risen this day!" This praise resonates in a way that brings down all the walls of sin, death, and the Devil.

Praise liberates the captives. As we read in Acts 16:16-36, we hear the story of Paul and Silas liberating a woman who was a fortune-teller. This woman was free from the bondage of sinful oppression. Paul and Silas were arrested, put in prison, where they were in stocks and chains. Even though they were physically bound, spiritually they were free. In their freedom, they praised God, and from that praise resonated an earthquake. The prison was broken, and they were now physically free. They did not leave, because they were free all along. In their freedom, they ministered to the jailer who was spiritually in prison. It was through Paul and Silas's proclamation of the gospel that he was set free.

The song of Jesus love and resurrection is the one that resonates from our hearts. It breaks the bondages of oppression and brings new life. Sometimes we can't get a song out of our head. We hear it over and over again. The songs of God's love and grace in Jesus Christ are ones that we meditate and sing all day. When we allow God's song of praise to rule in our hearts, our focus is on living the Christian life. We follow in the ways of God.

The Word Brings Peace

When we sing God's praise, we meditate on God's Word, our spirits are uplifted, and we give honor to God in all that we do.

When Mary received the good news, that she was going to be the mother of our Lord, she breaks into praise, "My soul doth magnify the Lord, and my spirit hath rejoiced in God my Savior." (Luke 1:46-47) To magnify something, means to make it as large and as great as we can. A magnifying glass will enlarge words. As we praise God, we are making his name the greatest in all the earth. It is one thing to speak God's word, and it is another to sing God's word. Our voices, our instruments, and applause, magnifies the Lord. We are communicating to God with all our might that he is the greatest, and we are thankful to God for whom he is and all that he has done. As the salvation of God entered into Mary, literally, it brought a song of joy to her. We also, who have been impregnated with the Word rejoice in the salvation of God.

As we read in Acts 3:1-10, we hear the story of a beggar. He was crippled since birth, and would sit outside the temple begging for money. Peter and John said, "We have no money to give you, but what we give you is the word of Jesus, "Walk." This man was able to go into the temple courts walking and jumping, and praising God. He was freed from his bondage to worship and praise God. When the Holy Spirit fills our hearts, we go into God's presence praising God in our singing, in our dancing, and making music to our God. We praise God for our freedom, healing, and new life.

As we read in 2 Samuel 6, as King David was able to defeat the Philistines, they were able to bring the Ark of the Covenant back to Jerusalem. In verse 5, "David and the whole house of Israel were celebrating with all their might before the Lord, with songs and with harps, lyres, tambourines, drums and cymbals." In verses 14-15, "David, wearing a linen ephod, danced before the Lord with all his might, while he and the entire house of Israel brought up the ark of the Lord with shouts and the sound of trumpets."

As the Apostle Paul writes, "But thanks be to God He gives us the victory through our Lord Jesus Christ." (1 Corinthians 15:57) A Christian life is one of praise to God for whom he is, and all that he has done.

A prayer of praise is one where we direct our adoration and glory to God. We experience the joy of worship.

It is one thing to speak God's word, and it is another to sing God's word. Our voices, our instruments, and applause, magnifies the Lord.

QUESTIONS

1. What makes you break out in praise?
2. What are ways that you praise?
3. How does praise make you feel?
4. What does Psalm 150 teach us about praise?
5. How does creation praise God?
6. What was the angels' chorus when Jesus was born?
7. What is your favorite hymn or spiritual song?
8. How does praise bring down evil walls in your life?
9. How does praise liberate you?
10. How does praise claim victory for you?

Prayer of Thanksgiving

A Thankful attitude will bring contentment and peace.

Thanksgiving is completing a blessing. God blesses us by giving himself to us. He gives us his person. He does this through creation. He has blessed us by creating us in his image. As we live life, we are a reflection of who he is. We have the ability to co-create, to think, to express, and to love.

God has given himself through his Son, Jesus Christ. We can identify with the words of the Apostle Paul, "I have been crucified with Christ, it is no longer I who live, but Christ who lives within me." (Galatians 2:20) God gives us salvation life.

As we read Revelation 19:1, 16, "Alleluia! Salvation and glory and honor and power belong to the

Lord our God...And He has on his robe and on his thigh a name written, King of Kings and Lord of Lords." The root word for worthy and worship, is worth. Jesus is the one who is worthy of our worship. In our worship, we thank and praise God. We declare Jesus as king, and give God all the glory.

We also put our worship into action. Our lives in society are a reflection of our worship. In Matthew 25:31-46, Jesus tells the story of his coming in his kingly glory, and he will be the one to cast judgment on the people. He will separate people to heaven and hell, like a shepherd that separates the sheep from the goats. Verse 35, "For I was hungry and you gave me food; I was thirsty and you gave me drink; I was a stranger and you welcomed me." Jesus identifies with the needy. I was once serving in an affluent city where there were many fancy restaurants. Wealthy people would dine in these ritzy places. As a young pastor, I heard that an owner was a professed Christian and would serve a homeless person a meal. I wondered about this, being the contrast with the rest of the patrons. One day, I met a homeless man who was hungry. I took him into this fancy restaurant and spoke to the Christian owner. I said, "This man is in need of a meal." The owner proceeded to set the man down at one of his tables with the linen clothes and fancy tableware. He treated this homeless person as a king. The man is one who honors Jesus as the king. Jesus is this man's worship and life.

God has given us his Holy Spirit, a life filled with blessing. Paul also writes, "Praise be to God and Father of our Lord Jesus Christ, who has blessed us in the heavenly realms with every spiritual blessing in Christ." (Ephesians 1:3)

God's blessings are his creative and redeeming favor upon us. When we give thanks to God, we are completing God's blessings. God shows his favor upon us through loving action, and we show our love to God by returning thanksgiving to God.

As God has shown us his unconditional love through Jesus Christ, we now show our love by giving our lives to God. What God wants in return is not a part of us, but rather our whole person. He calls us to pick up our crosses and to follow him. (Matthew 16:24) We pick up the cross of Jesus, when we commit our lives to him, and his loving service to others. There is a prayer that I have found meaningful in my devotional life, "Heavenly Father, we offer with joy and thanksgiving what you have first given us, ourselves, our time, and our possessions, signs of your gracious love."

So often when we think of giving to God, we think of giving a tithe or tenth of what we have to God. We can offer a tenth of our time and financial resources to God's service. This is important in keeping the work of Christ's church active in the world. In giving a tithe to God's church doesn't mean that we use the other 90% for selfish purposes. We can offer our talents to God. We offer our time to God's purposes and work. Time is our greatest commodity, because we have a limited amount of it. God wants our whole person's body, mind, and spirit. All that we have, and all that we are, we give to God in thanksgiving.

Thanksgiving is our life-style. We are to be about thanks-living. We give in our living. The Apostle Paul wrote, "Owe no one anything, except to love one another." (Romans 13:8-14) Salvation comes as a free gift, but yet we give our lives in thankful response to God. We love God by loving our neighbors, especially those in need. Jesus said, "When you clothe the naked, feed the hungry, visit the sick and prisoners, and when you welcome the stranger; you serve me." (Matthew 25:35-36)

When the fire is outside of the fireplace, it is a cursed thing. We must always keep God's blessings in the context for which they are given ... Blessings are not to be hoarded, but rather to be shared.

The prophet Micah said, "He has showed you, O man, what is good. And what does the Lord require of you? To act justly and to love mercy and to walk humbly with your God." (Micah 6:8)

Paul writes, "Do nothing out of selfish ambition or vain conceit, but in humility consider others better than yourselves." (Philippians 2:3)

These Bible verses demonstrate a Christian attitude that is formed by prayers of thanksgiving. It is an attitude of love, humility, obedience, and service to God.

Three Things About Thanksgiving

We live with the understanding that thanksgiving is a godly lifestyle. It is in this:

1) *We know whom to thank for the blessings.*

2) *We understand the context for which the blessings are given.*

3) *We are blessed so that we can be a blessing to others.*

I remember a person who was given a gracious gift anonymously from someone. He was very appreciative of the gift, but his frustration was, he didn't know whom to thank. As we live life in the most wonderful creation, it is good to know whom to thank for all the goodness. We thank God.

With thanksgiving to God, a person knows what context to put the blessings in. Christian people live their lives to God. They do not follow their own wills, but rather God's will. God's blessings are always put in the context of God's purposes. When blessings are not put in the context of God's purposes, then they become curses. A person who receives a blessing, but then uses it for selfish purposes, soon finds the blessing to be a curse. When the blessings are used for God's purposes, then the blessings strengthen the ministry and life of the church. God gives his blessings for his intended mission in the world. When a fire is in a fireplace, it is a blessed thing. When the fire is outside of the fireplace, it is a cursed thing. We must always keep God's blessings in the context for which they are given.

The third thing is when a person is thankful, they will always see themselves as being blessed to be a blessing. Blessings are not to be hoarded, but rather to be shared. When God called Abraham, God would bless Abraham so that he would be a blessing to others. (Genesis 12:2) There is the word giving in thanksgiving, so our offering thanks is always a giving of what God has first given us.

> *We show our love to God by returning thanksgiving to God ...When we have a loving relationship with the Heavenly Father, our lives are an expression of thanksgiving.*

Thanksgiving Bible Passages

Psalm 136 is a psalm of thanksgiving. There are many petitions that are followed by, "His love endures forever." The anonymous psalm writer is going through the history of Israel, thanking God for his steadfast love and guidance. The petitions point out how thankful God's people are for his presence with them. The petitions are thankful for the many times that God has acted in their history. God has shown his saving power and the many ways that he saves his people. The psalm writer is thankful for God's steadfast love that has sustained them through life.

If we were to write a psalm like 136, what would be our petitions of thanksgiving? We would be thankful for creation and the many resources God has given us. We would give thanks for the resurrection of Jesus from the dead, and the certain hope of eternal life.

As we read in *Luke 17:11-19*, we hear the story of Jesus traveling from the region from Galilee to Jerusalem. As he travels, he goes through the region of Samaria. There was a prejudice that people from the regions of Galilee and Judea had with the people of Samaria. As Jesus was passing through Samaria, he comes in contact with lepers from a leper colony. Leprosy was a very painful skin disease that would lead to death. This disease was physically painful as the disease would eventually eat the flesh right off the person's bones. The disease was socially painful, because the people had to be quarantined. They had to leave their families, their homes, their communities, and places of work. This disease was also spiritually painful because the person was considered unclean before God, and could not participate in any religious ceremonies. Lepers were considered to be God-forsaken people.

Prejudices no longer matter, for they were neither Jews nor Gentiles; Galileans or Samaritans, but rather they were lepers. Sickness levels the plain of prejudice. As Jesus was passing by, the only prayer they had was, "Lord, have mercy." This is our prayer. We all have the disease of sin, and the consequence of sin is death. As much as we may try to make an argument for our goodness, our entitlements, and our right practices, our only plea is one for mercy. Jesus showed mercy on the lepers by healing all ten of them. Jesus shows mercy on all of us by dying on a cross for our sins. Jesus told them, "Go show yourselves to the priest." It was the priest who declares people clean or unclean. It is by the priest's pronouncement of declaring them clean that they are able to go back into society, to their homes, their families, their communities, and are allowed to return to religious ceremonies. So it is with us, Jesus, the High Priest makes us clean, holy and acceptable before the judge being God. We have been washed clean by the blood of Jesus.

Of the ten lepers, only one of them returned to give thanks to Jesus. It was the Samaritan. The others wanted physical healing so they could go on with their selfish purposes in life. The Samaritan saw his healing as being more than skin deep, but rather a healing of the soul for godly purposes. The Samaritan was not only healed physically, but was also healed spiritually. He was made whole in Jesus Christ. The other lepers were healed physically, but still were sin sick, not seeing any godly purpose for their healing. For the Samaritan leper, the blessing of God went full circle through his thanksgiving. It is through his thanksgiving, that he was now living life for the glory of God.

It was this man's faith that made him well. He is

well because he has a relationship with God. His life is made whole and complete. He lives in a state of peace. I have known people who are physically well, but yet sin sick; while I have known people to be physically sick, but spiritually whole. Their lives are made complete through the life, death, and resurrection of Jesus.

We treat symptoms in life, such as physical illness, but the rudiment of life is what stems from the heart. When we have a loving relationship with the Heavenly Father, our lives are an expression of thanksgiving. The blessings of God are complete. The Heavenly Father loves us, and we love him. The loving relationship of God has been made complete.

When we have a joyful attitude, we are uplifted and we uplift others ... People will appreciate our joyful attitude. As a negative attitude will rub off on those around us, so does a joyous attitude rub off on others.

As we read in *1 Thessalonians 5:16-18*, the Apostle Paul has given very profound words to live by. In these short three verses, there are three points. He writes, "Be joyful always; pray continually; give thanks in all circumstances, for this is God's will for you in Christ Jesus."

The first key point is to be joyful. When we have a joyful attitude, we are uplifted and we uplift others. Joy comes as the Holy Spirit dwells in us. We experience the joy that only God's presence can give. Why go through life with a negative and cantankerous attitude, when we can be joyful? People will appreciate our joyful attitude. As a negative attitude will rub off on those around us, so does a joyous attitude rub off on others.

The second key point is to pray continually. When we pray continually, we are always in relationship with God. The life of God's will is always being exercised in our lives.

The third key point is to give thanks always. Thanksgiving is an attitude of life. We give our lives in loving gratitude to God. Why go through life malcontent and complaining? A thankful attitude will bring contentment and peace.

As we live in these key points, they give us a godly attitude and perspective in life. This attitude will turn our greed into generosity. The best antidote for greed is generosity. The best cure for a negative attitude is to be joyful, and have a godly attitude in life. The best way to combat complaining is through thanksgiving. When we give thanks, we count our blessings and we share our blessings. We no longer dwell on the things that we have to complain about in life, but rather our lives become a joyous thanksgiving to God.

A person once said to me, "I don't give thanks to God because I have earned all that I have!" We must remember that creation, life, and the ability to work are gifts from God. We must be thankful stewards of all that God has blessed us with. We bear the fruit of his goodness. God is looking for a harvest of thanksgiving.

As a farmer plants a field with seeds, the seeds sprout forth and they mature into a plant that eventually bears the fruit of a harvest. As God's love and grace shines upon us through the seed of God's Word, we too bear the fruit of the Holy Spirit. There is a harvest of thanksgiving for the gracious blessings God bestows on us.

The best antidote for greed is generosity. The best cure for a negative attitude is to be joyful, and have a godly attitude in life.

QUESTIONS

1. Do you agree that thanksgiving is completing a blessing?
2. How is thanksgiving a transformation of life?
3. How do we offer our lives in thanksgiving to God?
4. What are three things about thanksgiving to God?
5. If you were to write a psalm of thanksgiving, what would be some of the verses?
6. What did the lepers beg from Jesus?
7. What is our human leprosy?
8. What is our begging prayer to God?
9. How does God show mercy to us?
10. What are the three key points of 1 Thessalonians 5:16-18?

Prayers of Intercession

Intercessory prayers are prayers of love, looking outside of self, being concerned for the greater whole.

I will hear so many people say, "I believe in the power of prayer." These are people who have dedicated their lives to God, and see God working in their prayer lives. They can give so many testimonies of how God is working daily in their prayer lives.

These people are also connected spiritually with other Christian believers who pray. They have a spiritual synergy where they are praying for each other, and together, they can testify to the power of God working through their prayers.

I was working as a hospital chaplain, when one day I went to the nurses' desk to say hello to the charge nurse. She was normally a very mild mannered woman. Before I could even say hello, she said, "Pastor Jeff, pray for our patients!" I could hear her sad frustration as they had some patients die on her floor that day. She conveyed to me the urgent need to be praying for others, imploring God to intervene in a critical time of need.

I know a retired pastor who prays for over 700 people every day. He starts praying early in the morning, and finishes at midday. His calling is to be an intercessor of prayer for so many people. I have heard people say in their old age, "I can't do much for people anymore, other than to pray for them." Praying for them is the most important thing. In doing this we are calling upon God to be engaged with all those people we are concerned about.

Prayers of intercession are prayers for other people. These are prayers of love for the church, the community, and our neighbors. Intercessory prayers are prayers of love, looking outside of self, being concerned for the greater whole.

R. J. was a little boy whose parents were no nonsense people. They were very serious about all of their dealings, even going to church. R. J. on the other hand was a bit of a character and one day while the family was worshiping in church, R. J. started to act up. It didn't take long for his father to take him over his shoulder like a sack of potatoes and started carrying him down the center isle out of church. As this was happening, R. J. pleaded with the other worshippers, "Pray for me guys, pray for me!" It is good that R. J. has a community of believers that would pray for him at this time as well as all times. As Christians, we are a community of believers that support one another as we pray for each other.

As the church, we are the body of Christ, unified in Jesus Christ. As the church, we can say with conviction, "I am they, and they are me." We have a mutual oneness in the bonding of Jesus unifying love.

The beauty of the church is that together we can witness and celebrate the wonder of God working in our lives.

Jesus said, "I am the vine, you are the branches. If a man remains in me and I in him, he will bear much fruit apart from me you can do nothing." (John 15:5) Jesus is the life come down from heaven. He brings spiritual life to each one of us, just like a vine brings life to its branches. Branches are plural, meaning that we are a community of believers that are connected to Jesus as the church. Jesus gives us life to commune together. Jesus once again stresses the relationship that God has with us. He uses the word "remain", to show that we are connected to God and to one another as a community. As Jesus is in the father, so Jesus is in us, and we are in the Father. As the Holy Spirit dwells in us, God is in us. As the church, we are living branches that are healthy, forgiving, working together, strong together, and bearing spiritual fruit together, for the kingdom of God.

God blesses us with the salvation of Jesus Christ, as we hear the Word and receive the Holy Sacraments of baptism and communion. We remain in God as we pray. Prayer is the communication that allows us to remain in God and one another in a spiritual unity.

The Power of a Praying Community

We are the body of Christ. We gather at his banqueting table to receive Holy Communion. We eat of the same bread and drink of the same cup. Together, we are bonded as one body, united to God and each other. This is the spiritual bond of God that unites us in a heavenly union. Together, we receive the salvation life of God, and we are united as God's children. We are bonded in this spiritual union in Jesus.

I will hear believers say, "I can be a Christian apart from the church." When a Christian is a "Lone Pine", he misses out on the beauty of being connected to the Christian community. Lone Christians do not share in the joy of being together, nor do they have the concern for those who gather. The Holy Spirit is working in the faith community, being the network of spiritual connectedness. There have been many times when someone will call me saying, "I was praying and God laid it upon my heart to call you, sensing that there is something wrong." Sure enough, something was wrong. That is the power of prayer, working through the Christian church. God intended for all believers to come together to be the church.

I will not go golfing by myself, because I'm afraid

the time I do is when I will hit a hole-in-one. As I go to the clubhouse to share my good news with excitement, who will believe me? I wouldn't have a witness. The beauty of the church is that together we can witness and celebrate the wonder of God working in our lives. The church together can rejoice and have faith strengthened. When Jesus arose from the dead, he appeared to many people, so many witnessed his risen presence. One time he appeared to over 500 people. (1 Corinthians 15:6)

Thomas, one of Jesus disciples separated himself from the rest of the disciples. When the risen Jesus appeared to the disciples, Thomas was absent. (John 20:24) He missed out in the exciting celebration the others witnessed. When Thomas rejoined the disciples, it was then he too experienced the joy and celebration of the risen Christ. (John 20:28) When we gather for worship, it is a celebration of the risen Jesus. We don't want to miss out on what God is doing in and through his church.

As we watch the night sky, we can see the stars that are permanently in their places. This would allow sailors to navigate the ocean on a clear night. Once in a while, one can see a meteor shoot across the sky. Meteors are unpredictable, but spectacular. God uses the steadfastness of his Word to be a constant for us. As we pray, God guides us in life, much like the stars with the sailors. Once in a while, we will have a supernatural God moment that is spectacular. It is a miracle that takes place in our lives. These moments are unpredictable, but special when they happen.

So often people think that God only works through

the meteor events of life. They think that God works only through the supernatural, while God has nothing to do with the natural. When something supernatural happens we give God credit, but when the ordinary happens, we give other things credit. We must remember that God is working through the natural order of things. God is working through his steadfast Word to give us, sustain us, and guide us in life.

Prayer is not a mechanism of trying to control God or the person that we are praying for, but rather, it is asking that God's will and discernment may happen to others as it happens to us.

As a community of faith, God uses the church to continue his work in this world. I have heard many Christians say, "God does miracles." They see God only working through miracles, supernatural events. God does miracles, but we must also realize that God works through his natural created order. In prayer, God activates the church and uses the stewardship of humanity to bring healing to the sick, homes for the homeless, comfort to the lonely, food for the hungry, and relief to those devastated by natural disasters. God has blessed the church with various gifts and talents to be the working body of Christ in the world. (1 Corinthians 12:6) Just as a mechanic has a toolbox to go about his work, so God has the church to go about his. We are the hands, feet, eyes, hears, and mouth of Jesus body on earth. Some Christians are working on the front lines, while everyone else is praying for, encouraging them, and equipping them, to fulfill the work that God has planned for us to do.

The Apostle Peter wrote, "But you are a chosen race, a royal priesthood, a holy nation a people belonging to God, that you may declare the praise of him who called you out of darkness into his wonderful light." (1 Peter 2:9) God has called the church out of the darkness of death, and into his light of salvation. Jesus who was rejected by humanity has become the foundation of the church. God's people, who have been rejected by the world, have become God's very own elect.

We are called to pray for each other. Sometimes I wonder why we are to pray for each other, when God who is all knowing, knows the needs of people better than we know them. Am I to pray for John Doe down the street to alert God that he has a need, and then tell God how to fix John? I'm sure that God is very much aware of John Doe's needs and what needs to happen.

The church is a spiritual network of God's people. God works through the church. It isn't so much our alerting God to John Doe's problems, but it is God bringing us to a compassionate awareness of what is happening. God is making his church active in love. As

God is concerned about John Doe, he calls upon the church, inspires them, and empowers them to be active in ministering to John. As the church, we are continually calling upon God to provide all that we need: wisdom, love, patience, and resources as we minister to him. We pray to God, as we are partners with God in ministry.

God works through people in creation and also in salvation. God has always left a part for humanity to play in creation and life. This is the stewardship that God has given to humanity. God has blessed humanity with the seeds, soil, rain, and sunshine, but yet has given the part for the farmer to plant the seeds and harvest them. God has given to us healing, but has left the part for the physician to bind the wounds. God has given to us materials, but gives the part for the builder to construct infrastructure. God has given us wisdom, but has given the part for the teacher to instruct people.

As Christians, we share in our mutual rejoicing and suffering. When one rejoices, we all rejoice, and when one suffers we all suffer. (1 Corinthians 12:26) So it is with the church, God did not entrust his work for the angels, but rather to his people. God has blessed the church with the stewardship of his Word and Sacraments, calling followers, instructing others in the faith, and the Christian ministry in the world.

John Doe is a member of the body of Christ. We are together the body of Christ. When John hurts, we all hurt, and when he rejoices, we all rejoice. We are one with John, and he is one with us. When our right hand hurts, our whole body hurts. As a bonded community, we pray. As we pray, those bonds get stronger and stronger, and we experience the presence of God who brings healing.

Jesus prayed for others, and he calls us to pray. How God works through our prayers is a mystery of our faith. As people are praying for others, we can see the hand of God working in their lives. I can feel the affect that prayer has on my life when people are praying for me. I can feel the Holy Spirit coming over me, changing my attitude, my mind, and also the direction of how God wants me to go. Prayer is not a mechanism of trying to control God or the person that we are praying for, but rather, it is asking that God's will and discernment may happen to others as it happens to us.

When we pray, we are asking God in his infinite love, wisdom, and mercy to use each of us and all of us to be the answer to prayers as well. We pray to God for answers to prayers, but indeed God will often prompt us to be the answer to other people's prayers as well. "Dear children, let us not love with words, or tongue but with actions and in truth." (1 John 3:18) Prayers always lead to action. A praying community recognizes its mutual love for one another. A praying community has compassion to serve the hurting. A praying community recognizes the importance of each person's contributions to the whole. A praying community recognizes our strength is in each other.

Jesus' Intercessory Prayer

When we pray for others, we are standing in the gap with them. Jesus is the one who stands in the gap between God and humanity. Sin separates us from God.

There is an abyss that we cannot go across. We cannot reach God through good works, knowledge, social status, or ethnicity. It is God who comes to us in Jesus Christ. It is through his suffering and death that this chasm has been bridged. We now have access to God through our Lord Jesus Christ. (Romans 5:1-2)

A priest is someone who stands in the gap and pleads on behalf of someone. In John 17, we hear Jesus high priestly prayer. Jesus prays for three things:

The first thing that Jesus prays for is unity. He wants his church to be one with him. The Devil wants to come and divide us, but it is God's desire to bring us together in unity.

The second thing that Jesus prays for is protection from the evil one. The Devil comes only to steal and kill and destroy; I have come that they may have life, and have it to the full.

The third thing Jesus prays for is to sanctify us in the truth. Sanctification is to be made holy. God is holy and he makes us holy. "Be holy, because I am holy." (1 Peter 2:16) Holy means, to be consecrated in his blood, set apart for his purposes.

As Jesus prayed this prayer on behalf of the believers, so we pray for the believers to be one in the Holy Spirit. We ask God to protect us from the Devil's temptations to destroy our lives. We ask God to fill our lives with the Holy Spirit, so that we may grow in our faith in God. As we read in 1 Peter 2:5, we are to be the "holy priesthood" of believers, praying for each other.

I once ran a race that was 16.2 miles long. The race had a slogan that was a math equation: $10 + 10 = 16.2$ miles. How is that possible? If you add ten English miles and 10 kilometers (6.2 miles), it adds up to be 16.2 miles. Sometimes in life, we may not always understand God's work and plan. This is why we live by faith. We trust in God who knows the whole picture of life, from beginning to end. We don't always know why we are to pray for others, and we may even try to outthink God; but we are called in the mystery of faith to pray for others.

When we pray, we are asking God in his infinite love, wisdom, and mercy to use each of us and all of us to be the answer to prayers as well.

Paul's Seven Reasons for Intercessory Prayer

As we read in Colossians 1:9-12, Paul is praying for the believers. He prays for a number of things, and these should be the petitions that we pray on behalf of others.

1. *We prays that God's will be done.* That is one of the keys of prayer. We don't pray that "My will be done", but rather we pray that "God's will be done". We are not asking God to fit into our reasoning, but rather we pray that we can always fit into God's purposes and plans.

2. *We pray that God will bless the believers with spiritual gifts.* As we live in God's plan as the community of believers, we pray that God will bless us with the spiritual gifts to serve in his church. We pray for the Holy Spirit to fill our lives, and that God will give us every spiritual blessing in the heavenly places. Praying that God's will be done, and for the Holy Spirit to enter our hearts is key to being the church, the community of believers.

3. *We pray that God will grant us the wisdom to lead us into the right resources to help the church.* In Matthew 9:1-2, we hear of people carrying their paralytic friend to Jesus. As I mentioned above concerning the stewardship of creation and salvation, God is working through people to provide help in need.

4. *We pray that God will be glorified in our lives.* As Jesus healed a blind man in John 9, there was a

debate about whose sins brought blindness to this man, he or his parents? Jesus said, "Neither, but rather that God maybe glorified in the healing." Jesus said, "This is to my Father's glory, that you bear much fruit, showing yourselves to be my disciples." (John 15:8) We pray that we bring honor to God in all that we do in our lives.

5. *We pray that God will send labors into the world's vineyard to bear fruit.* Jesus said, "The harvest is plentiful but the workers are few. Ask the Lord of the harvest, therefore, to send out workers into his harvest field." (Matthew 9:37-38) The fruit that Christians produce are: A) Virtues- such as, love, joy, peace, patience, kindness, goodness, faithfulness, and self-control. (Galatians 5:22-23) B) Good works (Colossians 1:10) and C) Bringing people to salvation. (Hebrews 13:15)

6. *We pray that God will grant each believer strength and patience in times of suffering.* Jesus said, "Those who endure to the end will be saved." (Matthew 10:22) Suffering comes to all people, and it is a test of our faith. As Peter writes in 1 Peter 1:7, "These have come so that your faith-of greater worth than gold, which perishes even though refined by fire-may be proved genuine and may result in praise, glory and honor when Jesus Christ is revealed." Fire can either consume or it can refine. In times of suffering, God can use this as a refiner's fire to purify and strengthen the believer's faith that is more precious than gold.

7. *We pray for compassion.* Jesus shows compassion for the hurting. It is out of the cross that Jesus poured out his blood for us. "And we know that in all things God works for the good of those who love him, who have been called according to his purpose." Some of the most compassionate people are those who have suffered the most. It is from Jesus wounds that we are healed. (1 Peter 2:24) God took the most tragic event in the history of the world, Jesus crucifixion, and has turned it into the salvation for humanity. It is out of our wounds, that we can show compassion and healing for others.

"May the God of peace, who through the blood of the eternal covenant brought back from the dead our Lord Jesus, that great Shepherd of the sheep, equip you with everything good for doing his will, and may he work in us what is pleasing to him, through Jesus Christ, to whom be glory for ever and ever. Amen." (Hebrew 13:20-21)

A community of believers that prays together stays together. A church that prays for each other is a loving church. The Holy Spirit is moving through the prayers of the people, strengthening and bonding people through Jesus love. "Love does not delight in evil but rejoices with the truth." (1 Corinthians 13:6)

I was visiting with a married couple who had gone through major problems. The problems almost brought a divorce. What saved their marriage was prayer. They started praying for each other, and with each other. Their whole attitude changed. Their fighting words were changed to praying words. Praying to God turned their marriage around completely. Instead of cursing, they were now praising God. They said, "Here are three key points: 1. Have Jesus as your Lord and Savior. 2. Be into God's Word, because the Bible gives answers to all problems, if you are willing to study and search. 3. Spend time in prayer." This is good advice for couples, but they pertain to any relationships that we may have. Those who pray together, stay together.

St. James writes, "Is any one of you in trouble? He should pray. Is anyone happy? Let him sing songs of praise. Is any one of you sick? He should call the elders of the church to pray over him and anoint him with oil in the name of the Lord. And the prayer offered in faith will make the sick person well; the Lord will raise him up. If he has sinned, he will be forgiven. Therefore confess your sins to each other and pray for each other so that you may be healed. The power of a righteous man is powerful and effective." (James 5:13-16)

Prayers of intercession are to bring glory to God, as we see God doing his wonderful works in the lives of other people.

QUESTIONS

1. Why is it important to be connected to a community of faith?
2. Who is the vine, and who are the branches?
3. What does Jesus want us to produce?
4. Why is it important to pray for each other?

5. What is the mystery of intercessory prayer?
6. How does God activate the church through prayer?
7. What three things did Jesus pray for in his High Priestly Prayer?
8. What are the seven things Paul encourages the church to pray for?
9. What is the strength of a righteous person's prayer?
10. Who are you praying for?

Prayers of Supplication

God's blessings of answered prayer can be a process over a season of life, or even for the course of one's life.

A prayer of supplication is when we are requesting something of God. Our prayer requests are for concerns that we may have in our lives, such as: needs, hopes, and goals that we set for ourselves. "Do not be anxious about anything, but in everything, by prayer and petition, with thanksgiving, present your requests to God." (Philippians 4:6)

Jesus taught us to pray, "Give us today our daily bread." (Matthew 6:11)

Leaders in the Bible were praying to God for specific things. Moses prayed for a voice to communicate; Joshua prayed for courage; David prayed for forgiveness; Solomon prayed for wisdom; and Elijah prayed for rain. In reality, all of these people were in constant prayer. Every step of their lives were held in prayer.

Motivations

As we approach God in prayer we should never have selfish motivations.

1) *We are not to pray for things that go contrary to God's will.*

2) *We are not to pray for things that are self-serving and boastful.*

3) *We are not to pray for things that dishonor God and hurt his church.*

4) *We are not to pray for things that will hurt our neighbors.*

5) *We are not to pray to God in superstitious ways. Prayer is not a magic act, or an act of wishful thinking.*

6) *Prayer is not to be used as a way to lie or swear.*

7) *Prayer is not to be used as an attempt to manipulate God.*

As we have our dreams and visions for life, it is always important to pray for God's discernment. The Holy Spirit uses God's Word (the Bible) to help us discern his will. God will use the wisdom of other believers to help us discern his will. Some prudent questions to ask are:

1. *Is the goal I have in life, according to God's will?*

2. *Does this goal glorify God?*

3. *Does this goal edify and build up the church?*

4. *Is my goal, one that loves others through actions?*

5. *Does the goal comply with the gifts that God has blessed me with in life?*

"On one occasion an expert of the law stood up to test Jesus, 'Teacher,' he asked, 'what must I do to inherit eternal life.'" (Luke 10:25) This man saw religion as an obligation of works of the law and do's and don'ts. He was seeing a godly regiment that would have requirements for inheriting eternal life. He was looking for a minimal input for a maximum output. An inheritance is not something that is earned, but rather is a gift.

Religion to this point was a legalistic regiment of trying to fulfill what the law demands. Our flesh, weakened by sin cannot fulfill this requirement. Jesus fulfills the just requirement. "For what the law was powerless to do in that it was weakened by the sinful nature, God did by sending his own Son in the likeness of sinful man to be a sin offering. And so he condemned sin in sinful man, in order that the righteous requirements of the law might be fully me in us, who do not live according to the sinful nature but according to the Spirit." (Romans 8:3-4)

Religion is now a personal relationship with God the Father. The impetus is his love. Love is a verb. The love of God is concerned about abstaining from evil, but even more concerned about being proactive in doing what is right. When we love our neighbor, we no longer want to hurt our neighbors in anyway, but rather we have the passion to do what is right. The Holy Spirit is infused into our person, giving us the passion for living a godly life.

God does not want to be understood as any angry taskmaster, nor does he want his people to think that they are slaves trying to earn eternal life.

As we read in Galatians chapter 5, Paul gives two sets of fruits. The one set of fruits represent our sinful nature, "The acts of the sinful nature are obvious: sexual immorality, impurity and debauchery, idolatry and witchcraft, hatred, discord, jealousy, fits of rage, selfish ambition, dissensions, factions, and envy; drunkenness, orgies, and the like." (Galatians 5:19-21) The other set of fruits are that of the spiritual nature that is infused in us by the Holy Spirit, "But the fruit of the Spirit is love, joy, peace, patience, kindness, goodness, faithfulness, gentleness, and self-control. Against such things there is no law." (Galatians 5:22-23)

God does not want to be understood as any angry taskmaster, nor does he want his people to think that they are slaves trying to earn eternal life. God wants us to understand him to be a loving father, and we are his blessed children. It is living in the covenant of our baptisms, that we live in the salvation of God. No matter how hard a slave works, he will never be welcome at the master's table, and he will never inherit what belongs to the master. A child is one who is always welcome to the father's table, and will one day inherit as a gift what the loving father so graciously gives. Salvation is living in the covenant of our baptisms in relationship to God. As we live in this covenant, our lives are motivated by love. We are not asking for the minimal requirements, but rather as people of thanks, we love the Lord more and more. Jesus offered this man life, and he turned it down. The Apostle Paul writes, "For you did not receive a spirit that makes you a slave again to fear, but you received the Spirit of sonship." (Romans 8:15)

As we pray, the Holy Spirit is transforming our sinful nature into a spiritual nature. This is evidence of the Holy Spirit's work in us.

J.C. Penney walked by the Holy Spirit. He was thankful for his relationship with God, and he demonstrated a life of walking in the Holy Spirit. He used the blessings of his life to build a retirement center for Christian pastors and missionaries of all denominations who had no income or pensions. He prayed for God to give him a dream and a vision for his life. His life has now been a blessing for so many retired Christian servants. His life was not about minimal religious requirements, but rather an expression of love. A person who is inspired by God asks, "What more can I do?"

God is our Motivation

God is a Christians' motivation in life. The Holy Spirit empowers the church to be passionate about God, to be his people, and to do his work. It is God who inspires the believer's visions and dreams. "In the last days, God says, I will pour out my Spirit on all people. Your sons and daughters will prophesy, your young men will see visions, your old men will dream dreams." (Acts 2:17) The prophet Jeremiah shares words of encouragement to God's people, "For I know the plans I have for you. Plans to prosper you and not to harm you, plans to give you hope and a future." (Jeremiah 29:11) As we pray, God will give us his dreams and visions for life. As we have our dreams and visions, they become our goals that motivate us in life. As we pray about these visions and dreams, the time comes when they become a reality. The reality is evidence of God working through his people, and establishing his kingdom in this world.

Psalm 42:1 states, "As the deer thirsts for the water, so my soul thirsts for thee." Just as we need water to quench our physical thirst, so we need God to satisfy the thirst of our souls. We thirst for God and we desire to be in relationship with him above all others. Jesus said, "I am the bread of life. He who comes to me will never go hungry, and he who believes in me will never be thirsty." (John 6:35) Our first desire in life is to be in relationship with God. Our prayer life is always to be in fellowship with God and other believers. We always pray and seek after a relationship with God.

God Answers Prayer

Hannah was a faithful woman before God. She so much wanted to have a son who she could dedicate to the Lord's service. She wasn't able to have children. She made her request known to God. The day came when God allowed her to become pregnant. She gave birth to a baby boy and named him Samuel. She brought Samuel to the Tabernacle in Shiloh, and it was there he was dedicated to the Lord's service. Samuel became a great prophet and priest. He is the prophet who anointed David as King. God spoke, "Those who honor me I will honor, but those who despise me will be disdained." (1 Samuel 2:30)

God answers prayer. Sometimes the prayer is answered directly, other times it is answered in a way that will be revealed in the future. We may say, "Oh, I remember praying about that, and now I understand why the prayer was answered in that way." Then there are times when prayers are answered in certain ways, and we will never know why. This is why we walk by faith, because we have to trust that God knows what is best in situations, for reasons that will be unknown to us.

God answers prayer through his Word. So many answers to our prayers are found in the Word of God. There are answers to prayers as we hear the preacher speak. As a preacher, I will be praying that God will give me the words to speak. I don't know why God puts certain thoughts and ideas in my head. After the sermon has been preached, some people will come up to me saying, "God spoke to me through that sermon. You must have known what I have been struggling with." In honesty, I had no idea.

Sometimes God will answer by speaking to our hearts. We will know that it is God's will and answer to prayer, as long as it is in compliance to God's Word. I remember praying about certain ministry callings. I will know that it is God's answer to prayer, as I feel like a piece of metal being drawn into a magnet.

As Christians, we are not to see ourselves as individuals, but rather as a community of believers that God has called together ... As we develop our prayer life, we can hear God calling us to be the answer to someone else's prayers.

God answers prayer through the wisdom of trusted Christian friends. I remember times when I have been praying about something, and God will send someone who will start visiting with me. In the context of the conversation, the wisdom spoken was the answer to my prayers.

As we read in Luke 11:13, "If you then, though you are evil, know how to give good gifts to your children, how much more will your Father in heaven give the Holy Spirit to those who ask him!" God promises to give all people the Holy Spirit when they ask in prayer. The Holy Spirit is the breath of God living in our lives.

As children, we have requests that we present before our parents. Sometimes our parents grant our requests, and other times they do not. Even though our parents are not perfect, when they parent in love, they know what is good for us. They will grant or deny our requests on that basis. As Children, we didn't always understand, and sometimes we could even become angry with them when they wouldn't grant our requests. So it is with God, we have to trust that he is granting or denying our prayer requests based on his loving wisdom. One thing we do know, that God will always answer our prayer request for the Holy Spirit. As we live in relationship with the Holy Spirit, we continue to come alive spiritually. We grow and branch out in the ways and purposes of God. We desire God more and more, and we seek his purposes for our lives. God's purposes and desires are the ones that we implement into our lives.

Jesus said, "Believe me when I say that I am in the Father and the Father is in me; or at least believe on the evidence of the miracles themselves. I tell you the truth, anyone who has faith in me will do what I have been doing. He will do even greater things than these, because I am going to the Father. And I will do whatever you ask in my name, so that the Son may bring glory to the Father. You may ask me for anything in my name, and I will do it." (John 14:11-14)

Jesus Calls and Claims us to Follow

Jesus is the one who beckons us to follow him. Jesus is the one who calls us to ministry and mission in the world. When, we are called by God to do his work, his ministry, and his mission in life; God provides for all that we need to do that work. We can pray for God to equip us for his mission and purposes.

Jesus instruction for us in prayer is: 1. We pray that God's will be done. We are no longer maligned by sin to live our lives apart from God, but now we have aligned ourselves to live in relationship with God in all things. 2. We work for the praise and glory of God. As we work in God's kingdom, we are working to further his causes. We want all of our good works to point to God, and bear witness to his name. 3. We pray in Jesus name. Jesus is the one who has all authority in heaven and earth. (Matthew 28:18) Jesus name is above every name. It is in the name of Jesus that every knee shall bow and every tongue confess that Jesus Christ is Lord. (Philippians 2:9-11)

Jesus is the author of life, and we get our authority from him. He is the one who has the power over death and the grave. Jesus is the truth concerning all of life. Jesus is the gate to eternal life. As we pray to God, we pray with confidence, knowing that God answers all of our prayers according to his good will and purposes.

Persistent Prayer

We live in an instant society. Society has conditioned us to receive everything right now! I can order a hamburger at a fast food restaurant, and after one minute of waiting, I'm wondering, "What is wrong with the service?" When we are accustomed to receiving everything instantly, we learn to live in the moment. We judge the world and our lives in the perceived day, rather than to appreciate life as being a process. God does not judge life in a moment or a day, but rather through the course of a lifetime. God's blessings of answered prayer can be a process over a season of life, or even for the course of one's life. This is why it is important to be patient and persistent in prayer. "For his anger lasts only a moment, but his favor lasts a lifetime." (Psalm 30:5)

As we pray, we are to be persistent. Jesus tells the story of the persistent widow in Luke 18:1-8. The story is about a widow who is seeking justice from an unrighteous judge. The judge does not fear God, nor does he care about this widow, but the widow was persistent in pestering the judge. She wore the judge out and he granted her the justice she was looking for. This parable is to show that we are not to give up on the visions and dreams that God has laid upon our hearts and minds. More importantly, this parable teaches us that God does bring justice to all of our lives through his son, Jesus Christ. Jesus dying on the cross is the just requirement for our sins. He gives gracious redemption as a free gift for us to receive in faith.

Sometimes God gives us a quick "Yes" answer to our prayers, and other times he gives us a quick "No". We should not be discouraged when the answer to our prayers is "No", for in our prayers God gives us peace and acceptance of a "No". We trust that the "No" is for a reason. In life it isn't always for us to know why God answers our prayers the way he does. Other times, God puts us on hold. God does not always answer our prayers in the moment, but will be able to answer them in a future time. It is in those importunate prayers that God tests our faith, and also strengthens our character, building us up as his people. "For those who hope in the Lord, God will renew their strength." (Isaiah 40:31) As we pray, whether the answers are yes, no, or we are put on hold, we are always growing into a deeper relationship with God through prayer.

Jesus tells a similar story in Luke 11:5-8, this is about a man who has an unexpected visitor at night, so he goes to his friend's house asking for some bread. People lived in one room houses, so the family, and all of the animals would sleep in the home. If the animals were left outside, they would be stolen in the night. It would take time for a man to get his family and animals all settled down for the night, so they can get some sleep. The last thing he would want is to be disrupted in the middle of the night. Even this man who has now been disrupted in the middle of the night was willing to help this person in need, so God is willing to listen to our prayers, and provide for our needs.

Genesis 32:22-32, tells the story of Jacob at the Jabbok river wrestling with an angel all night long. It was at the end of the wrestling that Jacob was blessed. Jacob was a conniving person who cheated his brother Esau out of his blessing. Even though Jacob could fool his father Isaac and brother Esau, he could not fool God. It was over the course of many years that God was working to transform Jacob into a man of high integrity. If Jacob was going to be a patriarch of God's great nation, he would need to be a person of godly character. As Jacob was tested at the Jabbok river, he passed the test. God blessed him and transformed his life so much that he changed his name from Jacob to Israel. Jacob was a new person. When we pray, we may find ourselves wrestling with God over the course of a long period of time. We must engage in the spiritual wrestle with God, knowing that he is forming, transforming, and making us to be a godly person. It is in the wrestling with God, that our relationship with him deepens, our faith grows stronger, and we experience the blessedness of the Christian life.

Praying In Times of Need

When it comes to times of need, we pray that God would grant us the wisdom to understand what the issue is. After we have identified the issue, we pray that God would help us to discern the best option. After we have chosen the best option, we pray that God will lead us into the right resources to exercise the option. We then pray for courage that God will restore our lives, and we also pray that God will grant us peace in all circumstances in life. As we give our lives to God in prayer, he guides us through his Word. As we read in Psalm 119:105, "Your word is a lamp to my feet and a light to my path." As we read Proverbs 3:5-6, "Trust in the Lord with all your heart and lean not on your own understanding; in all your ways acknowledge him, and he will make your paths straight." Prayer is always leaning and trusting in God's good guidance.

We pray for rain, as well as other things, but we must realize that the natural order of God's creation happens. Most years we have favorable weather, but in the natural cycle of years; some years we may have drought, and other times deluge rain. This makes for very trying times. In these times, we pray for God to either make it rain or stop the rain. In these years, as we pray, God will grant us the wisdom, character, and persistence to weather these times. "After a long time, in the third year, the word of the Lord came to Elijah; 'Go and present yourself to Ahab, and I will send rain on the land.'" (1 Kings18:1)

Community of Faith

I was once pitching in a baseball game. I was determined to strikeout all the opposing hitters. After I had walked a few batters, my coach came to the mound and said, "Look behind you, you have all of your teammates that will get the opposing team out; so throw strikes." As I looked at my teammates, I remember thinking, "They are very good players; I need to trust in them." As Christians, we are not to see ourselves as individuals, but rather as a community of believers that God has called together. God has given us the church, so that we can rely on each other. God has given us the talents and resources to be the answer of many prayers. As we develop our prayer life, we can hear God calling us to be the answer to someone else's prayers. I am always amazed at the work God is able to accomplish as he calls and inspires his church to action.

I have heard prideful people say, "Christians are people who need a crutch in life." I have always interpreted this to be a negative statement. In actuality, everybody has hurts, everybody has troubles, and everybody faces challenges in life. I am always thankful for the help God and his church gives in times of trouble.

God placed a rainbow in the sky for Noah to see. This was a sign of God's salvation, peace, and restoration. It was a sign of the promise that God will not destroy the earth with a flood again. "I have set my rainbow in the clouds, and it will be the sign of the covenant for all generations to come." (Genesis 9:13)

The rainbow is a symbol of God's promises. We hear God's promise of always being with us (Matthew 28:20), his promise of forgiveness (1 John 1:9), and the promise of eternal life (John 11:25).

The rainbow is also a symbol of the church. The rainbow is a tapestry of all the colors. Each one of God's people is a color. The church is not a matter of people being black and white, hoping to conform to the color gray. Instead, God is working to take the color of each member and blending it into a rainbow. This is the power of God making this happen. A praying church is a rainbow of God's amazing people. We are a people (church) of faith, hope, and love.

In all circumstances give thanks to God, knowing that he is with us, guiding us in the good times and the tough times. When we live according to God's promises and plans, he takes all of life's experiences and redeems them for his purposes.

> *"What a friend we have in Jesus,*
> *All our sins and griefs to bear!*
> *What a privilege to carry*
> *Everything to God in prayer?"*
> **– What a Friend we Have in Jesus**

Questions

1. What are prayers of supplication?
2. What are some goals you have in life?
3. What are some bad motivations in life?
4. How do you struggle with "My will be done" vs. "God's will be done"?
5. What dreams and visions has God laid upon your heart?
6. Why do we trust in God's fatherly love and wisdom?
7. What does Jesus promise all people who pray for it?
8. In what context do we understand Jesus words, "Ask me for anything in my name and will do it"?
9. What does Jesus instruct us to pray?
10. Why is persistent prayer important?

Warfare Praying

It was homecoming my senior year of high school. On Friday morning as I got to school, there was a buzz going through the halls; our opponent had burned their school's initials in our field that night. They were making claim to our football field. That night we were able to defeat our opponent reclaiming our field. Satan wants to make claim of our person. As Satan tries to put his initials on our person, it is Jesus who brings victory. God reclaims us as his children, and places the mark of the cross upon us. This is God's loving signature. We belong to God.

Like any contest, there is an offense and a defense. As Christian people, we are on the defense against the temptations and attacks from the Devil. Some church buildings are built to look like a fortress. "I will say of the Lord, 'He is my refuge and my fortress, my God to whom I trust.'" (Psalm 91:2) God is our strong defense against the wiles of the Devil. Like a football game, there are two teams. There is God's team and Satan's team. Whose team are we on? God's team is the victorious one.

As Christian people, we are not to just hide in fear while the Devil runs rampant in society. The Christian people are to be of good courage, for Jesus has overcome the world. (John 16:33) We claim the victory in Jesus, and we are conquers through him who loves us. (Romans 8:37) As God's people, we are to be light shining into the darkness. We are to drive out all evil from our lives, our communities, and our world. "We are not to be overcome by evil, but we are to overcome evil with good." (Romans 12:12) The cross of Christ stands as a symbol of God's victory over sin, death, and the devil. It is an eternal victory that nobody can take away from us. Christian people are to go on the offensive, and bust down the Devil's gate, and drive out all evil. (Matthew 16:18) This is the power of the Holy Spirit working through prayer. The Holy Spirit builds up the courage and spiritual strength to confront the Devil and be victorious.

The Devil/Satan

There is a spiritual tug-of-war going on in our lives between God and Satan, the battlefield is our person. Both God and Satan are trying to make claim on our person. The intent of God is to bring life, while the intent of Satan is to bring destruction. Jesus said, "The thief comes only to steal and kill and destroy; I have come that they may have life, and have it to the full." (John 10:10)

The Devil's will for your life is to destroy you! The Devil is very powerful. He is like darkness. Apart from light, darkness is the most powerful force. We cannot wash darkness away with the most powerful detergent; we cannot blow darkness away with a stick of dynamite; and we cannot suck darkness out of the night with a powerful vacuum cleaner. There is only one power stronger than darkness, and that is light. When light shines in darkness, darkness vanishes instantly. All the darkness of the night cannot extinguish the smallest flame. The darker it is, the brighter light shines. "In him was life, and that life was the light of men. The light shines in the darkness, but the darkness has not understood it." (John 1:4-5)

As we pray in the name of Jesus, the Devil will flee away like darkness vanishing with the light. "Submit yourselves, then, to God. Resist the devil, and he will flee

As Christian people, we are not to just hide in fear while the Devil runs rampant in society ... We are to drive out all evil from our lives, our communities, and our world.

from you." (James 4:7) Here again, if we do not receive the light of Jesus salvation, the Devil is the roaring lion that can devour you. This is the power of prayer, God working in your life.

Satan is a liar and a deceiver who will go about his work appearing to be doing good. Satan is not the person with the horns and pitchfork, but rather he works in the way that the Apostle Paul describes, "And no wonder, for Satan himself masquerades as an angel of light." (2 Corinthians 11:14) Satan will use good "Religious" people to teach false teachings to the people. He will use good people and events to draw people away from hearing the Word, receiving salvation, and gathering with the community of believers. Ultimately, Satan wants to destroy everything that God has worked and planned for your life, "For the wages of sin is death." (Romans 6:23) Peter, one of Jesus closest disciples meant well when he heard the discouraging words that Jesus must go to the cross. He was doing all he could to convince Jesus otherwise. Jesus reply to Peter was, "Get behind me, Satan!" (Matthew 16:23) Jesus could interpret Satan's deceit through Peter's good intentions. Satan was working through one of Jesus closest friends to destroy the plan of God.

Who is Satan? He was once a lead or archangel who rebelled against God. As we read in Isaiah 14:12-15, "How you have fallen from heaven, O morning star, son of the dawn! You have been cast down to the earth, you who once laid low the nations! You said in your heart, 'I will ascend to heaven; I will raise my throne above the stars of God; I will sit enthroned on the mount of assembly, on the utmost heights of the sacred mountain. I will ascend above the tops of the clouds; I will make myself like the Most High.' But you are brought down to the grave, to the depths of the pit." Satan was able to have a third of the angels rebel and they are demons, "His tail swept a third of the stars out of the sky and flung them to the earth." (Revelation 12:4)

God and Satan are not equal. Satan is bound by space and time. God does not let Satan roam wild throughout the universe making the planets go out of orbit. Satan was created, and God will bring him to an end. Satan has been defeated through the cross of Jesus. God will finally throw Satan into the lake of fire. (Revelation 20:10)

How the Devil Works

"But I tell you that anyone who looks at a woman lustfully has already committed adultery with her in his heart." (Matthew 5:28) A flower has its three parts: roots, stem, and flower. The flower is something that we can see, while the roots are hidden, but yet it is all one flower. The flower does stem from the roots in the soil. This is the way our lives are. The Devil will put a thought into our hearts. If we do not get rid of that thought right away, it begins to stake root. As the thought takes root, we then nurture and feed that lust. It begins to grow like a stem and branch out. Finally, the hiddenness of the thought matures and flowers. It is at this time that we are committing the act of sin. This all happens as a process: temptation, nurturing the temptation, and acting out the temptation.

When this happens, we need to repent. We need to uproot the evil that has taken hold in our lives, and replace it with a spiritual cultivation. God wants us to be "Good soil." (Matthew 13:8) We pray that God will cultivate our hearts to receive his Word. His Word is a seed planted in our hearts and nurtured to maturity. We will produce the fruits of his spirit. This is the harvest that God is looking for.

Heaven and Hell

Jesus said, "When the son of Man comes in his glory, and all the angels with him, he will sit on his throne in heavenly glory. All the nations will be gathered before him, and he will separate the people one from another as a shepherd separates the sheep from the goats. He will put the sheep on his right and the goats on his left." (Matthew 25:31-33) There will be a final judgment day. Jesus will send his people, who have received him into heaven; while those who reject Jesus, he will send them to hell.

Heaven is God's eternal home. (John 14:2) As we read in Revelation chapters 21-22, heaven is described as a beautiful place where there will be no more sin, suffering, and death. We will live in a perfect unity with the Heavenly Father. The Devil will not be present in Heaven.

Hell is a place of torment. It is described as an eternal fire. (Matthew 25:41) Hell is the second death. (Revelation 20:14) God is not present in hell.

Hell is a real place. As we experience a foretaste of heaven in this life, we also experience a foretaste of hell in this life, with all the suffering of the world. The world is the intersection of heaven and hell. As God is real, living, and active in our lives, heaven is a real place.

We should not take it likely. We should not joke about Hell, or use it as an expletive. As we experience the reality of Satan's power, we call upon the name of the Lord. This is where we find our peace.

The good news of Jesus Christ is life. Jesus death and resurrection saves us from sin, death, and the Devil. God frees us from this bondage on earth, and also, saves us from eternal condemnation in hell. God has saved us from these awful things, but saves us for the abundant life we have in him. We are the delight of the Lord, and he wants us to grow in our relationship with him, until the day when we are brought into God's heavenly home. God saves us to be his church of faith, hope, and love.

Jesus' Baptism

Jesus was baptized by John. It was then that God spoke saying, "This is my beloved son with whom I am well pleased." (Matthew 3:17) Jesus has the identity of being the Son of God, he was given the value of pleasing God in obedience to all that he commanded, and he was given the purpose of being the Lamb of God to take away the sins of the world.

Jesus' Temptation

Following Jesus baptism, the Holy Spirit led him into the wilderness for a time of testing. Jesus was in the wilderness for forty days. Adam was in a perfect relationship with God, until he was tempted by the Devil.

(Genesis 3) Adam and Eve fell to Satan, the deceiver. Sin entered into their lives and in turn, has entered into humanity. This is humanity's condition. Our sinful actions are symptomatic of our human nature that has been set apart from God. Jesus is the "Second Adam, or first born." (1 Corinthians 15:47) Like Adam, Jesus goes through a time of testing. For Jesus to be the Lamb of God to take away the sins of the world he had to be sinless or what Levitical law would refer to as a sacrificial lamb without spot or blemish. The animal had to be perfect.

In the forty days that Jesus was in the wilderness, he did three things: 1. He fasted. 2. He prayed. 3. He meditated on God's Word. After forty days, you would think that Jesus would be weak and easy prey for Satan. Instead, Jesus was strong in the Lord. When we fast before God, we fast for a purpose and we show that we are committed to being obedient to God. In this case, Jesus was fasting to completely empty himself before God, and be filled with the Holy Spirit. There is godly power and strength in the Holy Spirit working through the Word.

Satan comes before Jesus with temptations. He said, "If". "If" is used as a word to bring doubt. Satan says, "If you are the Son of God", trying to instill doubt of Jesus identity as the Son of God, his godly value, and the purpose for his life. The devil is trying to destroy the plan that God had for Jesus.

The first temptation that Satan brought before Jesus is one of material value to satisfy the body. Satan said, "If you are the Son of God, turn these stones into loaves of bread." This seems like the obvious temptation, you would think that Jesus would want to turn the desert into a bakery. The temptation is to disobey God, and satisfy one's personal physical needs and desires. Jesus said, "Man shall not live on bread alone, but on every word that comes from the mouth of God." (Matthew 4:4) Jesus used the Word of God to show that life is made manifest solely in relationship with God, and not of the things of this world. God, not Satan is the source of all physical needs.

The Second Temptation had to do with entertainment. The Devil said, "Go to the top of the temple and throw yourself down, for the angels will come to save you." The Devil uses the Word of God in tempting Jesus to use his divine power to do things that are not of God. It is tempting to take Bible verses out of context to rationalize sinful purposes. Jesus said, "Do not put the Lord your God to the test." The temptation is to impress people. If you can do something spectacular, people will follow you. We enjoy our entertainment and those who entertain us. Jesus could have gained much fame for the moment, but like all entertainment, the excitement fades away.

I hear Christians say, "You don't have to go to worship to be a Christian." "You don't have to serve God to be a Christian." "You don't have to have fellowship with believers to be a Christian." My question to these Christians is always, "If you don't have to be a Christian to be a Christian, why be one?" God is ultimately the judge of who is Christian, but I would not put him to the test. I have also known Christians to use Bible verses to justify sinful behavior.

The third temptation has to do with power. The original sin was to be God, so the thought of ruling nations and the world is a temptation that the Devil will test Jesus with. The Devil said, "I will give you all the kingdoms of the world if you worship me." The Devil is a liar, the nations of the world are not his to dole out. Jesus said, "Away from me, Satan! For it is written, 'Worship the Lord your God and serve him only.'"

Jesus would not misuse his powers. Some of the darkest periods of human history are a result of atrocious leaders misusing power. Jesus used his power solely in the context of living in obedience to God's purposes.

Worshipping God is our greatest strength against temptation. When we worship, we pray for God's lordship in our lives. When we fail to worship God, then we dedicate our lives to other things that become our idol gods. This leads to Satan's dominion in our lives. The Old Testament is the history of God's people Israel. This history shows when God's people failed to worship God, they fell into depraved living, and eventual defeat. When they worshipped God, they were strong and healthy people. They were people filled with the joy of God's salvation. "Let us not give up meeting together, as some are in the habit of doing, but let us encourage one another." (Hebrews 10:25)

Jesus passed the test; he did not fall to the temptations that the Devil set before him. What we learn from this lesson is that we too will be strengthened as we fast, pray, and meditate on God's Word.

The Cross

The story of David fighting the great Philistine warrior Goliath is recorded in 1 Samuel 17. David, being a youth took his sling and five stones, and went down into the Valley of Elah to fight Goliath. Goliath was the most feared warrior being nine feet tall. David having the confidence of God being with him was able to slay the giant.

Jesus carried the cross as he went to Golgotha taking on the Goliath of sin, death, and the Devil. He had nails driven through his hands and feet, and a sword that pierced his side. In the resurrection, he gained victory over this Goliath. It is by his five wounds that we are healed.

People experience purpose in life when they serve. A servant's life will have a great impact on the lives of others.

Fellowship and Serving

Two other things that will help us be strong against the Devil are fellowship and serving. Jesus had to go down the path to Jerusalem on his own, but it is strength for us to journey through life with other believers. It doesn't take much strength to break a toothpick. It may not take much strength to break two toothpicks, but if you put enough toothpicks together, pretty soon you cannot break them. So it is with a Christian who surrounds himself with other believers. "As iron sharpens iron, so one man sharpens another." (Proverbs 27:17) The church is the product of the Holy Spirit. It is the Temple of the Holy Spirit. As the church grows strong in faith, it drives all evil out of its presence. As Jesus said, "Not even the gates of hell can prevail against it." (Matthew 16:18) The church will not only be strong in defense of evil, but will be offensive to knock down its gate and gain victory over it.

In a world of selfishness, a generous servant is light shining in the darkness. They make our world a brighter place.

The other way that Christians can be strengthened in faith is by serving. A person who serves, experiences the joy of God's presence. We are yoked with Jesus as we serve. People experience purpose in life when they serve. A servant's life will have a great impact on the lives of others. They are making this world a better place. Their contributions have a ripple effect that expands deep into society. Their work will be a legacy that will be influencing the lives of others for generations to come. God builds up believers to be giants in the faith, and their work is monumental.

It is when we teach the Word of God, we grow in the Word; and the more you grow in the Word of God, the more you will want to teach the Word. The more that people do good works for others in the name of Jesus, the more they grow in faith; and the more they grow in faith, the more they will want to serve. This becomes a spiritual cycle of faith that strengthens the believers.

As we pray, God transforms our thinking, our attitudes, and our approach to life. As we pray, our hate turns to love, revenge to forgiveness, negativity turns to positivity.

When we know whose we are, our value, and our purpose in life before God, then it is easier to say, "No" to Satan's desire and will for our lives. The Apostle Peter wrote, "Be self-controlled and alert. Your enemy the devil prowls around like a roaring lion looking for someone to devour. Resist him, standing firm in the faith, because you know that your brothers throughout the world are undergoing the same kind of sufferings." (1 Peter 5:8-9) Being self-controlled is a fruit of the Holy Spirit. It is having spiritual discipline in all matters of life. When a person is not defined and having self-control, it is easy for Satan to derail this person from living for the purposes of God.

The Armor of God

The Apostle Paul gives instruction on spiritual warfare in Ephesians 6:10-18, he says, "Put on the full armor of God." (Ephesians 6:11) Paul who was in prison when he wrote this letter, was probably looking at a Roman soldier who was guarding his prison cell. He uses each piece of equipment to describe a strength that God gives us.

Belt of Truth In ancient times, people wore long flowing robes. If a person wanted to be free to move, they would tie a cincher around their waste to hold up their robes. This gives them the freedom to move. This is what truth does, it gives us the freedom to move and live. Jesus is the truth about what is right from wrong, what is true from what is false, and what is good from what is bad. When we live in the truth, we live free from guilt and we have nothing to hide. Jesus said, "If you hold to my teaching, you are really my disciples. Then you will know the truth, and the truth will set you free." (John 8:31-31) Jesus is the truth that sets us free from the bondages of sin, death, and the Devil. We can speak and live boldly knowing we are living in the grace and promises of God. We live in the freedom of Jesus Christ.

Breastplate of Righteousness All things proceed from the heart. We pray that God will continue to create in us righteous hearts and that the Holy Spirit will dwell within us. (Psalm 51:10) It is spiritually vital that we pray for forgiveness and the Holy Spirit's presence to dwell within us. As Jesus said, "For out of the heart come evil thoughts, murder, adultery, sexual immorality, theft, false testimony, slander." (Matthew 15:19) We need the righteousness of God to protect our hearts at all times.

Shoes of Peace It is written in Isaiah 52:7, "How beautiful on the mountains are the feet of those who bring good news, who proclaim peace, who bring good tidings, who proclaim salvation, who say to Zion, 'Your God reigns!'" In ancient times, a messenger would bring the news by foot; normally the message was bad news. The message was often one of war. On a rare occasion the messenger would bring a good news message of peace. Peace is a spiritual state that God wants all of us to have. God wants us to be at peace with him, and with each other. King David wrote, "Peace be within you." (Psalm 122:8) Jesus said, "Peace I leave with you, my peace I give you. I do not give to you as the world gives. Do not let your heart be troubled and do not be afraid." (John 14:27) The Apostle Paul wrote, "And the peace of God, which transcends all understanding, will guard your hearts and your minds in Christ Jesus." It is with our feet that we bring the good news of the gospel to the world; it is a message of love, peace, and joy to the world. Christian believers have the greatest news to share.

The Shield of Faith A shield protects us from things that can hurt physically. Temptations come before us from all directions. It is by loving God and following in his commandments that we have boundaries to protect us. God has given to us his laws to create guidelines and order for our lives. We put our faith in God who gives us spiritual perspective in life.

The Helmet of Salvation The head is the most important part of our body. It is something that we need to protect. We wear helmets as we play football and ride our bikes. God gives us the salvation of Jesus Christ to secure the victory against the condemnation of sin, death, and the power of the Devil. In God's salvation our minds are transformed by the power of the Holy Spirit. Our mind is where our thinking is. The rest of our person will follow that thinking. Just like a snake, the body will follow the head. We must always put our mind on the salvation of God, his Word, and keep our focus on him. We live what we believe, so we must be careful what we focus our minds on.

As we pray, God transforms our thinking, our attitudes, and our approach to life. As we pray, our hate turns to love, revenge to forgiveness, negativity turns to positivity, and our enemies become our friends. This is the power of God working through our prayers.

The Sword of the Spirit The sword of the Spirit is God's Word. It has its two edges. One edge is the law of God's Word that brings judgment upon us, but the other edge of God's Word is the gospel, the good news that in Christ we are forgiven and set free. It is the Holy Spirit that searches the very depth of our hearts, and brings us to confession and forgiveness. In the Word of God, we proclaim salvation to those who receive Jesus, and condemnation to those who reject God's gracious offer.

In Luke 8:26-39, is the story of Jesus encountering a man who was possessed by demons. This man had so many demons that he is called "Legion". This shows that if we fail to repent of our sins, this condition like anything else will grow. Sin has matured in this man's life to where he is out of control.

In verse 28, the demon says, "What do you want with me, Jesus, Son of the Most High God?" The demons are theologically correct from the standpoint they know who Jesus is. Jesus is God in human flesh. People have debated who Jesus is over the years, ironically the demons know who he is, and they know Jesus is the only one who can destroy them.

Christians confess Jesus, the incarnate Son of God. As we pray, the Holy Spirit becomes incarnate in us. We begin to be transformed from the inside out.

The second thing about the believers is they obey the commandments of God. "God is love. Whoever lives in love lives in God, and God in him." (1 John 4:16) As Christ dwells in the believers through the Holy Spirit, our lives become an expression of God's love. We begin to mirror Christ's love in the world, even though it is a dim mirror. (1 Corinthians 13:12) It is Jesus who fulfills what the laws demand. As people love God and their neighbors, they abstain from doing what is evil, and are empowered to do what is the godly good.

The third thing about faith is that we must trust to follow Jesus in the ministry of carrying the cross. The cross represents the victory of Jesus that we all now share. The cross represents forgiveness, reconciliation, and new life. It is also through the cross that we bear witness to Jesus in all that we do.

Pray to Forgive Others

The Devil wants us to hate each other, and bring destructive actions that hurt, that oppress, and destroy others and humanity. The Devil wants to divide and conquer humanity.

When we hurt others, we want to feel justified in doing so. We have a right to our actions. The original sin is to be God, so we feel that others are pawns on our life's Chessboard. When others hurt us, we feel that we have a right to retaliate and get even. As we throw our angry stones, it does nothing but destroy society. We find ourselves as a humanity winning battles to ultimately losing the war.

God has a different method to iron out differences and bring peace. It is called forgiveness. It takes a stronger person to forgive than to fight. It is by God's love that we are given such strength. We pray that we can forgive others. Jesus said, "But I tell you: Love your enemies and pray for those who persecute you." (Matthew 5:44)

Forgiveness is unnatural to our human nature. Forgiveness is a gift of God. When Jesus was dying on the cross he said, "Father, forgive them, for they do not know what they are doing." (Luke 23:24)

We are to be reconciled to those who hurt us. The Apostle Paul writes, "All this is from God, who reconciled us to himself through Christ and gave us the ministry of reconciliation." (2 Corinthians 5:18)

Jesus said, "Greater love has one than this, that he lay down his life for his friends." (John 15:13) We are to make friends of our enemies.

If a hunter goes out into the jungle and kills a lion, we may say, "He is strong!" What would we say of a person who goes into the jungle and comes out with a tamed lion? We pray that we may have an attitude of love and peace. We want to work to heal and restore relationships.

Surround yourself with other believers who share the same values that you do . . . Keep steadfast in God's Word . . . If you fall, don't let the Devil make you feel defeated

As we pray, we recognize that Jesus paid the ultimate sacrifice for us. Because of Jesus love, we have forgiveness, reconciliation, and a relationship with God. When God has forgiven us our insurmountable debt that we could never pay, we can forgive our brothers and sisters of their debts; they are small in comparison. Jesus tells a parable to this effect. (Matthew 18:21-35)

When we forgive, we are giving up our "perceived

right" for revenge. It takes two to fight. Instead of returning harm to our neighbor, we do good for them. It is hard to hate someone who does nice things for us. We come to recognize that this isn't my enemy but my friend.

When we are at peace and have friendships with others, all people prosper. When people are feuding or at war, nothing productive is happening. Nations that build friendships, are nations where both prosper.

God's ways always bring blessings. People need to try God's ways, and see the blessed results. It takes persistent prayer in our lives for this attitude to come to fruition.

Pray for the Salvation of People

Jesus said, "The harvest is plentiful but the workers are few. Ask the Lord of the harvest, therefore, to send out workers into the harvest field." (Matthew 9:37-38)

The biggest battle is over the peoples' hearts. Who makes claim on us. God wants claim on us, but the Devil also wants claim. The Devil is working hard to get people to turn away from God, and live their lives for him. The Devil wants to destroy. God is working to bring people to his salvation. God uses his church to bring people to salvation. God is calling us. How does he do this? Here are five ways that God can use us to claim battleground, as people come to his Lordship:

1. *We pray that God will use our example of living the Christian life.* When you are a person of joy, peace, and hope; that is attractive. When you are

a person of wisdom that is attractive. When you are a person who makes your faith active in love; that is attractive. When you have a persevering character during times of adversity; that is attractive.

In the early church, people did not self-proclaim themselves as Christians. People who were followers of Christ were given that nickname. In other words you were accused of being a Christian. Being called a Christian was an honor, because he was bearing Jesus name, and also there was enough evidence that would indicate that he was a genuine follower of Jesus.

2. *We pray that God will give us the courage to invite our non-believing friends to church.* We need to offer opportunities for spiritual growth and fellowship. When we offer these opportunities, we then invite people to have fellowship and friendship with us. We are always to welcome the stranger in our midst and show hospitality. (Hebrew 13:2)

3. *We pray that we can engage in loving dialogue with unbelievers.* Listen to their stories. What is it they are saying? What are their interests? What are their goals? What troubles are they facing? What are their aspirations for the hope of the future? What are some of the stumbling blocks of having a strong faith?

4. *We pray that God will use our testimony to bring people to salvation.* What is your story of faith? How did you come to salvation? How is God active in your life? Share your testimony; it is genuine. How can people argue against the transformed life?

5. *Pray that God will use our serving as a witness to the unbeliever.* When people see the outpouring of your life to others, they will see Jesus in you. Jesus poured out his life for us, and we now pour out our lives for others. In a world of selfishness, a generous servant is light shining in the darkness. They make our world a brighter place.

   The Christian church is about developing relationships with each other. When people have a love for God and one another, there is a connectedness that fulfills the human need to be loved and included.

6. *Pray that God will help us be strong witnesses to unbelievers through our suffering.* God will build in us endurance, character, and hope. The unbelievers watch how we handle times of adversity. I knew a man who suffered from Multiple Sclerosis. He was a great example of God working a strong faith in his suffering.

7. *In these end-times, we pray that we will show a confident spirit of love, joy, and peace.* We live with the certain hope of the resurrection and life to

come. A Christian who loves and serves others in the end-times is a bold witness of Jesus.

Steps to Warfare Praying

1) *Remember your identity as being a child of God.* You find your value and worth in God. Do not compromise that value.

2) *Pray in the name of Jesus.* He is our mediator between God and us. It is by his authority that the Devil flees, and you are cleansed of all evil.

3) *Fill your life with the Holy Spirit.* When the Holy Spirit resides in you, there is not room for the Devil to set up shop.

4) *Surround yourself with other believers who share the same values that you do.* Be accountable to them, confess to them, and confide in their prayerful wisdom. Avoid people who want to bring you down.

5) *Keep steadfast in God's Word.*

6) *If you fall, don't let the Devil make you feel defeated,* but rather confess your sins and claim the victory you have in Jesus.

7) *Keep your mind on God.* You do this when you are prayerfully meditating on the Word of God.

"Go to dark Gethsemane all who feel the tempter's power;
Your Redeemer's conflict see.
Watch with him one bitter hour;
Turn not from his griefs away;
Learn from Jesus Christ to pray."

– Go to Dark Gethsemane

QUESTIONS

1. Do you believe that Satan is real?
2. How does Satan try to bring you down?
3. Do you feel the tension of good and evil in your life?
4. Who is Satan?
5. What did God say at Jesus baptism?
6. What were Jesus temptations?
7. How do you like Paul's illustration of the Roman Soldiers gear?
8. What do the demons refer to Jesus as being?
9. What are the steps to warfare praying?
10. How does God defeat Satan?

Praying the Path

*Even in the most difficult
times of life, God is working
his good . . . prayer is best
learned when practiced.*

"But small is the gate and narrow the road that leads to life, and only a few find it." (Matthew 7:14) "He guides me in paths of righteousness for his name's sake." (Psalm 23:3) Jesus is the path that leads to eternal life. It is the righteous path that isn't always the easy path, but always the blessed path.

A father took his three children on a hike up a mountain path. The one child hiked up a short distance and reported to his father. The father asked, "What did you see?" The child said, "I saw beautiful animals." The second child had hiked half way up and came down. The father said, "What did you see?" The child said, "I saw some beautiful trees." The third child hiked all the way to the summit and came back down. The father asked,

"What did you see?" With great excitement he said, "I was able to look across the vast valley and river, and see the new land!" This is what the Father wanted all three of his children to see.

God wants all of us to enjoy the wonderful experiences of this creation and life. What God wants us to see is his heavenly kingdom. It is by prayer that God guides us down the path of righteousness, and gives us a glimpse of his eternal glory in heaven. As we get a glimpse of heaven, we now see all of creation and life in a different way. We see the spiritual significance of God's creative work in it all. As we journey in life, we journey toward home. Life has a final destination.

Prayer is being in relationship with God. As we pray, we want to align ourselves with God. We want to be in synchronization with God's plan, promises, example, and work. God has created us to be in fellowship with him, and be in harmony with creation.

God from the very beginning of creation has history moving toward a great finale. As there is a beginning, there is also an ending. As the Apostle Paul writes, "Being confident of this, that he who began a good work in you will carry it on to completion until the day of Christ Jesus." (Philippians 1:6) With God there is not only a starting line, but also a finish line. With God we know where life is heading and ending, and the ending is also the beginning of a new life with God in heaven.

As a marathon runner, many runners are at the starting line. The marathon course is very long, but yet it has a lot of beautiful sights and interesting things along the path. We can get caught up on the journey, looking at all the interesting things, that it is easy to lose sight of the finish line. As we are journeying we may become despondent thinking, there is no finish line. The finish line is out there, and in crossing the finish line, there is a celebration. It isn't who is at the starting line that counts, but rather, who makes it to the finish line. We all must be encouraging each other to have the endurance to finish life's race. We must also know that the saints before us are also cheering us on. "Therefore, since we are surrounded by such a great cloud of witnesses, let us throw off everything that hinders and the sin that so easily entangles, and let us run with perseverance the race marked out for us." (Hebrews 12:1)

The frustration with humanity is that we have fallen to sin. We were aligned with God's providential care, but now have been maligned and out of control. Humanity is no longer operating according to God's script, but now is operating on an unknown script. The script will end in condemnation. This script leads to destruction and hell. It is like humanity being on a raft heading down a rushing mountain river towards a waterfall. The point being that sin leads to death. Sin as it matures, progresses, and evolves will eventually destroy itself. As humanity is on this cataclysmic course, Jesus died for us. He is there to rescue us before we go over the waterfalls.

In the 1980's there was a three-part movie, "*Back To The Future.*" It is a story of a scientist who invented a time machine. They go into the past with the time machine, and then they go into the future with it. As they do this, if they tamper with anything in the past or the future, it will have an impact on the course of history or the time continuum. This is what has happened with sin, it has put us on a time continuum or a path that is different than the one that God has set for humanity. Instead of being on the righteous path that leads to eternal life, we are now on a destructive path that leads to death. Jesus who is God in human flesh, descended from heaven and got on our time continuum, he dies for our sins, ascends back to the eternal time continuum, and now places those who receive Jesus on the righteous path of life. (Philippians 2:6-10)

Jesus said, "Enter through the narrow gate. For wide is the gate and broad is the road that leads to destruction, and many enter through it. But small is the gate and narrow the road that leads to life, and only a few find it." (Matthew 7:13-14) The path of destruction is very wide, but the righteous road is narrow. God doesn't give us a time machine to correct the past and guide our future, but rather, he has given us Jesus, the savior who forgives our past, and promises a hopeful future. Jesus is the narrow road.

God gave his original blessing to be in a perfect relationship with him, with humanity, and with creation. The original sin was the desire for humanity to be God. Through the sacrificial love and grace of Jesus, we have been brought back into the original blessing of being a child of the Father.

As we read John 14:1-6, we hear one of Jesus promises, the purpose of the promise, and the instruction of the promise.

The Promise- "Do not let your hearts be troubled. Trust in God; trust also in me. In my Father's house are many rooms; if it were not so, I would have told you. I am going there to prepare a place for you." The promise is that in Heaven there is a place for you. Jesus prepares as many rooms as people who receive him. In ancient times, when a son got married, the father would build another room for his son and bride to dwell in. He would build as many rooms as needed. Heaven is not like a game of musical chairs, but rather there is the promise that God prepares a place for you. In receiving Jesus, there is the assurance of knowing that when we die, there will be a place in God's heavenly home for us. God's time continuum culminates in heaven, there will be more rooms than a large inner city hotel. The vacancy sign of the Father's house is shinning bright. Jesus light shines in our world for all to see.

The Purpose- "And if I go and prepare a place for you, I will come back and take you to be with me that you also may be where I am." (John 14:3) The purpose is that God wants to be with us always. God desires a relationship with us more than anything. Just as God wants a relationship with us in this life, so it is God's desire to be with us in the next life. Nothing can separate us from the love of God in Christ Jesus our Lord. (Romans 8:39)

The Instruction- Thomas, one of Jesus disciples didn't understand what Jesus was saying, and was wondering how do we get to this place? Jesus said, "I am the way and the truth and the life." (John 14:6) How do we get to heaven? What path do we take? Jesus is the way to heaven; he is the righteous path. We do not need a compass or a map, or in this modern day, a GPS. In faith, we cling to the hand of Jesus. "He guides me in paths of righteousness for his name's sake." (Psalm 23:3) Jesus is the right path. He is the one that leads to eternal life. All of humanity is at the starting line, but is there a finish line? There are many paths in life, but they all end up as dead ends, except the path of righteousness.

"Now faith is being sure of what we hope for and certain of what we do not see." (Hebrews 11:1) Hope is not wishful thinking; it is the certainty of what God has promised. The Holy Spirit makes us certain of the hope we have in Jesus Christ.

"Do you not know that in a race all the runners run, but only one gets the prize? Run in such a way as to get the prize." (1 Corinthians 9:24) All who run in faith, will gain the prize of eternal life, but being a follower of Jesus does take endurance because of the spiritual warfare the Christians are under. Jesus said, "All men will hate you because of me, but he who stands firm to the end will be saved." (Mathew 10:22)

Jesus is the Way

"A highway shall be there, and a road, and it shall be called the highway of holiness." (Isaiah 35:8) The road to heaven is in our hearts. As we journey through life, God makes himself manifest in our hearts. God promises eternal life, Jesus is the way to God, and it is the Holy Spirit that makes us holy. As we journey through life toward the heavenly home, God's salvation dwells in us. The heavenly path is a spiritual path. It is our spiritual path that guides our physical path.

The way of Jesus is the way of the cross. Once

again, Jesus way isn't always the easy way, but it is the blessed way. Jesus suffering and death on the cross has paved the way to eternal life. We too, are to pick our crosses and to follow Jesus. (Matthew 16:24)

As Christians, we walk down the righteous path, and as we do, we become righteous. We continue in the Word of God. "Your word is a lamp to my feet and a light for my path." (Psalm 119:105) As we walk down the righteous path, we are following Jesus. He knows the way. It is not for us to determine the path. We put our faith in following Jesus, he will lead us to the heavenly home. We are to trust in God to make the next step in life. God gives us the light to take the next step, as we study and ascertain God's Word. While camping, I will walk on a dark path at night. It is my flashlight that gives me enough light to make my next step. That is what the Word of God does for us.

As we go down the righteous path, we grow in righteousness. We grow and become more in the likeness of Jesus Christ. God builds us up in this journey of life, that we may bear the fruit of a Christ-like person. The Apostle Paul wrote, "I press on toward the goal to win the prize for which God has called me heavenward in Christ Jesus." (Philippians 3:14) As Christians our goal is heaven, but yet the goal in this life is to be more like Jesus. We will never reach the perfect beauty of the savior in this life, but we make it our aim to be more like him every day.

Jesus is the Truth

We have been lied to. The devil would like us to believe there is no God of creation, there is no point to life, and all there is to live for is my selfish life with all of its passions and desires. This attitude makes humanity depressed, it has nothing to hope for. People have a negative attitude toward creation, life, and those around them.

God gives us the truth of creation, as we are given the stewardship of it. We no longer see the separation of creation and humanity, but rather now we are to be the caretakers, seeing the unity between God, humanity, and creation. We see the truth about sin and its consequences. We know the truth of God's plan of salvation in Jesus Christ. We obey the truth of God's command as being the measure and standard of what is right from what is wrong. We live in the truth of God's promises concerning eternal life.

It isn't who is at the starting line that counts, but rather, who makes it to the finish line. We all must be encouraging each other to have the endurance to finish life's race.

Jesus is the Life

It was from the ground that God formed Adam and breathed life into him. (Genesis 2:7) In sin we have death. In the resurrection, Jesus breathes spiritual life into us, "And with that he breathed on them and said, 'Receive the Holy Spirit.'" (John 20:22) The breath of Jesus is the Holy Spirit. We receive heaven's breath and resurrection life. God's breath is powerful and transforming in our lives. We will experience life in a new and beautiful way. Life will take on a fullness that will be beyond anything this world can give.

"Then Jesus declared, 'I am the bread of life. He who comes to me will never go hungry, and he who believes in me will never be thirsty.'" (John 6:35) The life of Jesus is abundant and full, "I have come that they may have life, and have it to the full." (John 10:10) We also know that the life of Jesus is eternal, "For God so loved the world that he gave his one and only Son, that whoever believes in him shall not perish but have eternal life." (John 3:16)

As we journey toward home, God gives us the joy of his presence. Life is special. As we pray, God brings an abundant richness to our relationships. We enjoy the beauty of the earth. We have a passion for the work that God has called us to in vocation, community, and service. God brings a splendor to our journey. With God, we experience life to its fullest!

Returning Home

In Luke 15:11-32, Jesus tells the story of a lost son. He was living in the covenantal relationship with his father. A covenant of being a child of the father, an inheritor of what the father would eventually give him, and a place in the father's house. The son rebelled, went off to a far away land, where he squandered his father's wealth. The son was way off the path. When the son came to his senses, he went back to his father, repenting of all that he had done. The father received him back.

As we live in the covenant of our baptisms. We are children of God, have our home with the heavenly father, and will inherit eternal life. As we may stray from our spiritual home, we must remember that God loves us and want us back. God is gracious and forgiving. We know that we are at home, when we are home with God. We have the peace of living in his house.

> "Amazing grace! How sweet the sound,
> That saved a wretch like me!
> I once was lost, but now am found,
> Was blind but now I see."
> **–Amazing Grace**

A Stewards Prayers

The question gets asked, "What do we pray for?" Jesus said, "He causes his sun to rise on the evil and the good, and sends rain on the righteous and the unrighteous." (Matthew 5:45) A devout Christian may ask, "Why does the rain fall on my atheist neighbor's fields?" Should we pray since God blesses everyone with what they need whether they are believers or not? This has to do with the first order of creation. God has created the universe and has given it order. Everything works like clockwork. God has given to humanity the stewardship of taking care of the earth. For the sake of creation and humanity, it is important that it rains on the Atheists' fields. Humanity needs the Atheists' fields to produce food for the world. Humanity is dependent on each other for community and survival. If blessings of creation and life only happen for the believers in this world, humanity will not be able to survive.

In Matthew 13:24-30, Jesus tells the parable of the wheat and the weeds. When the stewards were wanting to uproot the weeds, Jesus said, "Let them grow up together, because you do not want to damage the roots of the wheat." God will separate and judge on the final day. We pray God's blessings upon all humanity, for God needs to work his creative purposes in this world.

This goes with the big question of why doesn't God rid the world of all sin and evil? If this is what we are praying for, we are asking God to wipe out all of humanity, and that includes ourselves. God doesn't come to wipe us out, but rather comes to save us. God is always showing his love and mercy to us. God is always working to transform and make us into a new creation. The Apostle Paul writes, "Therefore, if anyone is in Christ, he is a new creation, the old has gone, the new has come!" (2 Corinthians 5:17)

Make a list of all the things that you are praying about. Sometimes we may not see God working in a day, but over time as we look back over the prayer list ...

We pray so we can be in relationship with God. The sun is going to shine whether we pray for it or not. The Kingdom of Jesus comes whether we pray for it or not, but I can appreciate what Martin Luther says, "But we pray that it will come to us."

A life of prayer is always a life dedicated to loving God. It is a life where we are seeking his will, and looking outside of ourselves in serving him and our neighbors.

The second order of creation that we pray for is Jesus coming into our lives. Jesus does not barge into our lives, but rather he knocks on the door, "Here I am! I stand at the door and knock. If anyone hears my voice and opens the door. I will come in and eat with him, and he with me." (Revelation 3:20)

We have been maligned by sin. We repent and ask God to come into our hearts, and realign us to his providential will. We, who have been on a track heading for a derailment, have now been placed on the track that leads to life. This is where we live under God's providential care. When we refuse to open the door, the rain will come, but the salvation of Jesus doesn't; and we are on the cataclysmic path of destruction. When we pray for the kingdom of Jesus to be enthroned in our hearts, we now align our lives for the purposes and glory of God. We no longer have the selfish desires of, "My will be done," but rather we pray, "God's will be done"; we align our lives with God's heavenly and creative purposes for this life.

A Prayer List

A prayer list or journal is important to keep. Make a list of all the things that you are praying about. Sometimes we may not see God working in a day, but over time as we look back over the prayer list, it is always exciting to see how God answers prayer. As we walk down the path of righteousness, it is something to see how God has been guiding us by prayer. We can rejoice in seeing how God has answered our prayers according to his will. We see our lives being transformed and taking on great meaning. We entrust our lives to God who sees our whole life from beginning to the end. Jesus said, "I am the Alpha and Omega, who is and was, and who is to come, the almighty." (Revelation 1:8)

A life of prayer is always a life dedicated to loving God. It is a life where we are seeking his will, and looking outside of ourselves in serving him and our neighbors.

Even in the most difficult times of life, God is working his good ... Some of the most compassionate people, who have made the biggest ministry impact are those who have suffered the most.

Conclusion

God does not want to be a puppeteer, but rather he wants a relationship based on love. When we shut God out, we cannot blame God for the awful things that may happen to humanity. It was not God who ate the forbidden fruit; that was humanity's decision. When we love God, God allows us to live, move, and have our being in him. This does not mean that bad things will not happen to us, but we must remember that God will work good in all circumstances. (Romans 8:28) Even in the most difficult times of life, God is working his good. God can now redeem all of life's experiences for his life-giving work. God does not desire for us to get bad diseases, have accidents, and broken relationships, but even in these times, we pray that God will enter into our life situations. God will use these situations to develop endurance, character, and hope in our lives. God will take adverse situations to strengthen us. God will give us compassion, wisdom, and opportunities to minister and strengthen other Christian believers according to the redemptive plan that he now sets for us. Some of the most compassionate people, who have made the biggest ministry impact are those who have suffered the most. God once predestined all believers to receive eternal life, but now because of sin, this life is for those who call upon his salvific will. God has placed blessing and curse before us, as well as, life and death. We want to choose God who brings life and blessing. (Deuteronomy 30:19)He brings to us eternal salvation. This happens because the Holy Spirit of God dwells within us, "And he who searches our hearts knows the mind of the Spirit, because the Spirit intercedes for the saints in accordance with God's will." (Romans 8:27)

It was during the Jewish Passover Festival that Jesus was crucified and rose from the dead. It was at the Jewish Pentecost Festival that God gave the Holy Spirit. There was a third festival, the Festival of Booths. This was a festival of the harvest, a time to give thanks. It was also a festival commemorating their time in the wilderness when they lived in tents. They were nomads wandering in the wilderness with the hope and promise of entering into the Promised Land. We journey through this wilderness with the certain hope and promise of entering into the Heavenly Promised Land.

We are waiting the completion of this journey, when we can celebrate the harvest of souls on the day of Jesus Christ, when God will bring his people home. This is the day that we prayerfully long for. We await the heavenly festival, where we no longer will live in our earthly tent, but be given a new body, a new home, and a room that Jesus has prepared for us in heaven! (2 Corinthians 5:1; John 14:2)

Pray, "Come Holy Spirit!" Amen. Remember, prayer is best learned when practiced.

QUESTIONS

1. What is intriguing about a path?
2. With God, where is life heading?
3. What has gotten humanity off the path?
4. Why is the righteous path difficult?
5. How does God put us on the righteous path?
6. Why is truth so important?
7. How is Jesus the life?
8. Why does God allow the rain to fall on the unjust?
9. Why would a prayer list be helpful?
10. How does prayer make a relationship with God possible?